Frontispiece:

On 5 November 1630 the Treaty of Madrid ended the war between Britain and Spain which had broken out in 1624 after the renunciation of the treaty for the marriage of Prince Charles (later Charles I) and the Spanish Infanta. The peace treaty was ratified on 7 December 1630. This illustration shows the Spanish copy now in the Public Record Office which was exchanged during the ratification process (SP 108/465).

PUBLIC RECORD OFFICE READERS' GUIDE NO. 7

NEVER COMPLAIN, NEVER EXPLAIN:
Records of the Foreign Office and State Paper Office 1500-C.1960

by

Louise Atherton

PRO Publications

PRO Publications

Chancery Lane

London

WC2A 1LR

©Crown Copyright 1994

ISBN 1 873162 13 8

CONTENTS page

Acknowledgements

I should like to express my thanks to the following for their advice in the writing of this short guide: Dr Mandy Banton, Dr Amanda Bevan, Mr C D Chalmers, Dr Meryl Foster, Mrs Hilary Jones, and Mrs Alexandra Nicol.

I am also particularly grateful to Dr Elizabeth Hallam Smith, Mr James Murray, Ms Fiona Prothero, Mr Melvyn Stainton and Mrs Marion Edwards for their advice, encouragement and technical expertise in the production of this work. I would also like to thank Mr Gerry Toop, Mr Brian Carter and Mr Richard Elvin for their help in producing the illustrations.

Any inaccuracies remaining in the text are, of course, the sole responsibility of the author.

Louise Atherton
January 1994

1. Introduction

There are innumerable sources for the study of foreign relations in the early modern and modern period in the Public Record Office (PRO). This guide is intended as a general introduction to the most important record classes, namely the state papers foreign and the records of the Foreign Office. It is intended as a guide for first time readers and those researchers wishing to expand their work into new areas. It should be of particular value to new postgraduate students working in a particular field of foreign diplomacy and needing a general introduction to relevant sources held in the PRO. There are some hints about the use of these records by genealogists, although it must be stressed that their value for family history research is fairly limited. Besides describing the various types of records, this work attempts to provide insights into how to go about research into the sources held in the PRO, with practical guidance on the state papers and using the nineteenth and twentieth century systems of Foreign Office filing and registration. It cannot, however, due to the limitations of space, pretend to be a comprehensive guide. It does not examine the sources for the study of colonial policy. Nor is it a guide to foreign policy sources which are scattered throughout other record classes in the PRO or those available outside, although, where appropriate, information is given on how to find locations of relevant material in other classes and repositories.

Most records relating to foreign affairs in the early modern period can be found in the state papers foreign and the state papers domestic, which cover the period c. 1500 to c. 1782 and are held at Chancery Lane. The records of the Foreign Office, held at Kew, are the main sources for modern diplomacy from c. 1782, although earlier papers are included amongst them. Other sources for early modern and modern foreign policy include the papers of private individuals, of which the PRO has a number of deposited collections, private office papers, records of the Exchequer and the Treasury (for the financial aspects of overseas policy), the Ministry of Defence and its predecessors (for British naval, military and air policies overseas) and the Privy Council and Prime Ministerial and Cabinet records (for discussion of foreign policy at the highest level). The PRO also holds a variety of transcripts of material held in archives overseas. The following work lists some of the major record classes available as well as providing a very general introduction to the nature of foreign policy making from the sixteenth to the twentieth centuries.

2. Medieval and Early Modern Diplomacy

Before the rise of the nation state, medieval Europe was governed in theory by the concept of the unity of Christendom. In practice Europe was made up of kingships, overlapping sovereignties, both secular and ecclesiastical, and feudal hierarchies. The making of foreign policy was usually the preserve of the king and his closest advisers. There was no exchange of diplomatic representatives between defined states as we know it in the twentieth century. Embassies could be received from the vassals of a particular lord or from princes or prelates. These representatives could be sent on behalf of the emperor, popes, princes, provinces, corporations or cities, and were appointed for individual and usually precisely defined missions.

There were many different names for diplomatic representatives in the medieval and early modern period. By the fifteenth century attempts were made to define the status and powers of emissaries. In 1436, in his *Short Treatise About Ambassadors*, Bernard du Rosier, later on archbishop of Toulouse, stated that the terms ambassador and legate were really two names for the same office, but in practice they were usually applied to secular and papal envoys respectively. For minor business and representation, two types of agent developed. The first was the nuncio, who acted as a messenger or courier, speaking for a principal or authority, but with no powers to negotiate. The second was the procurator, with specific legal power to negotiate and represent the principal. During wartime, the ceremonial heralds took on quasi-diplomatic functions, as the bearers of ultimatums and warnings. But these terms and offices were not used consistently, and there was confusion until the seventeenth century when the term plenipotentiary was invoked more frequently to denote envoys with legal powers to negotiate.

It was rare for an envoy to receive written instructions before the fifteenth century. As the level of diplomatic activity increased, however, it became more usual for instructions to be issued. By the sixteenth century there was often a formal set for the scrutiny of the receiving power and a private set for the ambassador alone. It also became usual for the state to defray the costs of the envoy during his journey. These expenses could be very large and not all were refunded by the government, which meant that diplomatic embassies were usually carried out by those with large private means.

The evolution of the idea of permanent representation between two authorities came about as a result of the rise of national states in Renaissance Italy. States became conscious of their boundaries; some refuted the overlordship of the pope and many found it necessary to contract alliances for security. To remain aware of developments in neighbouring and often rival states, representatives were assigned abroad on semi-permanent missions, to conduct routine business and to provide information. This was, however, very much a gradual development amongst the European states.

Much information was also gathered from the merchant communities abroad. The expansion of trade fostered the concept of representation; merchants required representatives to safeguard their interests in foreign lands, and from this need evolved what we know in more recent times as the consular service. The first state to develop consular representation was Venice, and its example was followed by trading companies in the fifteenth and sixteenth centuries. In the case of England, the interests of the Levant Company in the Ottoman Empire were defended by an 'ambassador' appointed by the company. The gathering of information was also facilitated by the rise of European banking, with its branch network for the flow of funds which could serve equally for the transfer of news.

By the 1450s, most states had chanceries and organised methods of diplomatic reporting. Specific rules for the form of despatches were developed by 1500. Such despatches often included transcripts of documents, either legitimate or intercepted, or contained information and observations based on reports of informers or others. Ambassadors began to employ secretaries, who were given responsibility for more routine work, but the envoy was generally expected to provide an analysis of the political situation, assessments of the leading statesmen and politicians, and sometimes a 'relation' on the termination of the mission, the most famous being the *relazione* of Venetian envoys. In the case of England, lack of formal reports at the termination of a mission suggests that these assessments were made orally, although a few written reports are scattered throughout the state papers foreign.

During the fifteenth century, as an alliance system evolved outside Italy, the greater European powers began to use ambassadors more frequently. But envoys were not appointed in a regular manner and there was no structured diplomatic service. Moreover, the state could be, and often was, reluctant to provide adequate financial backing. The development of diplomatic archive keeping and organisation was similarly uneven. The religious differences of the sixteenth and seventeenth centuries also meant that Catholic countries usually dealt only with other Catholic countries directly, and Protestant with Protestant, which tended to narrow diplomatic contacts. After 1589, Elizabeth I maintained diplomatic relations only with protestant powers, the Huguenot king of France, the Netherlands and the Ottoman Empire. Those attempting to bridge the divide could be linked to heresy and disaffection, and were often accused of spying.

However, by the late seventeenth century most of the great powers exchanged permanent embassies, with the exception of the Ottoman Empire which did not maintain representatives in Christian Europe until 1793. Envoys could still be appointed for specific missions and it was not uncommon to find smaller states sharing representatives. Ambassadors were usually appointed to capital cities - for example, Paris, Rome, Venice, Vienna - with lesser officials and merchants dealing with consular affairs.

Most of the pre-1500 records of diplomacy in the PRO consist of the expenses of envoys, diplomatic correspondence and transcriptions of treaties. There is very little material for this period which shows how decisions were arrived at by those who had responsibility for the formulation of policy, but there are transcriptions or notes of decisions which were made to record a precedent, treaty or law. In the late medieval period the question of foreign policy involved the king and most of the great departments of state and there was no recognised department for foreign affairs. Thus, the Chancery might be involved in the drafting and recording of treaties and diplomatic agreements upon its existing forms of documentation, while the Exchequer or the Wardrobe would include the expenses of missions in their formal accounting systems. In the case of the financial aspects of diplomacy this remained true of much of the early modern period, and some details of diplomatic interest could be recorded on the Patent rolls, for example letters patent of appointments. The real development of the early modern period in archival terms is the growth of personal correspondence between the domestic government and the overseas representative and the provision of more effective communication routes both in England and on the Continent.

Records of medieval origin which continue into the early modern period may often contain relevant information and can be used in conjunction with the state papers. Some of the chief sources are as follows:

C 76 Treaty Rolls, 19 Henry III to 26 Charles II

This is a composite record class, containing enrolments of treaties, letters and diplomatic material, 1234 to 1675. The rolls were kept up to the eighteenth century, but the later ones have not survived. Many of them concern the administration of French territories, apart from Gascony. For the texts of later treaties, readers should consult the relevant classes in the state papers foreign at Chancery Lane and the relevant Foreign Office classes at Kew. (See sections 5.4, 5.5 and 15.1). Treaties may also be enrolled on the Patent rolls (C 66), the Close rolls (C 54), the Gascon rolls (C 61), the Scotch rolls (C 71) and the Roman rolls (C 70). Some of these classes can be referred to using the following printed calendars: *The Calendar of Treaty Rolls*, 2 volumes, covering 1234-1325 and 1337-1339; *The Calendar of Close Rolls*, (56 volumes, covering 1227 to 1509) and *The Calendar of Patent Rolls* (72 volumes, covering 1216 to 1578).

E 30 Diplomatic Documents, Henry I to James I

A collection of original treaties, ratifications, agreements, abstracts, marriage treaties and settlements with some documents relating to foreign loans, [1103] to 1624. Other documents include powers given to foreign ambassadors to treat, notarial attestations, royal letters, letters of protection and safeconduct, leases, petitions, exemplifications and opinions of the universities touching the king's marriage, 1529 to 1530. These records are listed in more detail in the PRO *Lists and Indexes* volume XLIX.

E 36 Treasury of Receipt: Exchequer Miscellaneous Books, Edward I to George II

Pieces E 36/186-192 contain diplomatic documents, Edward II to Henry VIII, which mainly concern English possessions in France while E 36/191 contains material relating to the marches of Scotland and Wales in the time of Henry VIII. E 36/192 includes instructions to ambassadors at the court of Aragon, again for the reign of Henry VIII, and there are also copies of treaties and diplomatic documents in the *Registrum Munimentorum*, known as Liber A and Liber B, covering the period from King John to Edward I (E 36/274-275). Many of the books for the reign of Henry VIII are calendared in the *Letters and Papers* series (see section 6.1).

E 101 King's Remembrancer: Accounts, Various, Henry II to George III

This class includes the original accounts and vouchers for the expenses of ambassadors, nuncii and other persons attached to them on missions abroad (mainly 36 Henry III to 13 James I, 1251 to 1616), and receipts of the accounts of Calais, Henry VII to Philip and Mary. This class also contains accounts and administrative documents relating to English possessions in France. The *praestita*, or accounts of vouchers or imprests issued for the king's service, also include the accounts of messengers sent abroad.

E 351 Pipe Office: Declared Accounts 1500 to 1817

Pieces E 351/43-52 include the accounts of expenditure of ambassadors and envoys, 1545 to 1706. E 351/530-535 include treasurers' accounts for Calais, 1542 to 1545, and E 351/1273 contains details of the sale of Dunkirk in 1662.

E 403 Exchequer of Receipt, Enrolments and Registers of Issues, Henry III to 1834

E 403/2420-2429 include payment books for the Privy Purse, which provides accounts of the wardrobe, household and ambassadors, 1571 to 1593.

DL 34 Duchy of Lancaster: Ancient Correspondence and Diplomatic documents, Henry I to Elizabeth I

This class contains a few documents relating to the early modern period. DL 34/1533-1545 includes safeconducts and permits for the queen of Scots.

KB 33 Court of King's Bench: Crown Side: Precedents and Miscellaneous, c. 1600 to 1907

This class includes examples of libels on foreign sovereigns. The records are mainly those of indictments against individuals and journals for defamation of foreign rulers and their representatives, 7-15 George II (KB 33/5/9). A copy of the offending article or newspaper may be included.

SC 7 Papal Bulls, [1131]-1533

Documents in this class refer to international ecclesiastic and diplomatic matters, and include letters of protection, orders, confirmations of sentences, collations, monitions and exhortations to prelates. After 1500 this class includes papers relating to Wolsey's appointments and powers to negotiate in international conferences, for example in the League against the Turks in 1518. These records are listed in more detail in PRO *Lists and Indexes* volume XLIX.

Many medieval and early modern treaties, diplomatic papers and letters can be found in Thomas Rymer's *Foedera, Conventiones, Literae...* (first published in London, 1704-1717, and the Hague 1739-1745, with an incomplete edition by the Record Commissioners, 1816-1869). This work contains copies of documents from 1101 to 1654 which are now in the British Library, the PRO and other repositories. Where these are held by the PRO a reference is usually given, but these are in an older form and may be difficult to locate in the modern referencing system. Nonetheless the work provides a useful collection of important documents, the majority of which are in their original Latin.

3. The Office of the Secretary of State in England and the conduct of Foreign Affairs, c. 1500-1782

In England the king's secretary was often employed in the medieval period on diplomatic missions. The secretary was first formally appointed in 1377, as the keeper of the private seal. The role and responsibilities of the secretary evolved during the fifteenth century, and Edward IV usually kept two secretaries, using one for diplomatic missions. Gradually, the secretary started to take responsibility for the gathering of foreign and domestic intelligence and began to attend meetings of the Privy Council. With the appointment of Thomas Cromwell as secretary in 1534, the office took on new significance in the council, parliament, and in domestic and foreign affairs generally. But the secretary depended very much on royal favour as the fall of Cromwell illustrated. In 1540, due to pressure of work, two secretaries of state were appointed. Their powers were, in theory, identical.

By the mid sixteenth century the two secretaries of state controlled the routine work of foreign affairs. They received reports from and issued directives to English representatives abroad and dealt with foreign envoys in England. During the appointments of Cecil and Walsingham, the secretaries built up a formidable network of secret agents for intelligence gathering. But the secretaries' role was not comparable to the modern role of the foreign secretary; both also had responsibility over domestic affairs, particularly in local law and order, prevention of political disturbances, and in domestic intelligence. They also played a large part in the presentation of papers and information to the Privy Council. The secretaries did not have settled responsibility for particular countries and their representatives until 1640 when a geographical division of duties was made. This became permanent after 1660 when the secretaries began to be called formally the secretary of state for the Northern Department and the secretary of state for the Southern Department. The Southern Department dealt with the mainly Catholic countries, including France, Italy, and Iberia as well as the Ottoman Empire and Switzerland. The southern secretary also had oversight of the colonies, Ireland and the Channel Islands. The Northern Department dealt with the protestant countries - the German states, Holland, and Scandinavia, as well as Poland, the German Empire and Russia. Until the early eighteenth century the Southern Department took seniority, but the position was reversed with the accession of the Hanoverian George I with his interest in German politics and northern diplomacy in 1714.

The secretaries could and did manipulate their control of foreign affairs for political motives and professional rivalry. The office was not necessarily linked to political ability, and before the beginnings of accountabilty to Parliament in the eighteenth century and the development of party, was awarded by royal patronage.

The early seventeenth century saw a relative decline in the quality of secretaries who were chosen not so much for their professionalism as for their courtly status. Tenure, which depended on royal favour, was uncertain and did not provide political continuity. Courtly life also demanded an envoy well graced in the social and ceremonial arts, and there was less tendency for lawyers or professional men to be posted to positions abroad than there had been in the Tudor period. Envoys now tended to deal with less important negotiations as a matter of routine and there was more emphasis on the protection of fellow countrymen abroad. Appointments were made on the basis of patronage or purchase, and the ambassador's or envoy's entourage resembled a personal household rather than an administrative unit.

The post-Restoration period saw an expansion of the secretaries' work in foreign affairs. They gained more control over the issue of passports, which had previously been signed by the king himself. The foreign secretary obtained the sole right to issue passports in 1794. The secretaries also tended to dominate the restoration committees on foreign affairs. They continued to have a role in military policy, acting as intermediaries in the making of appointments and the issuing of news and instructions to commanders. The appointment of the secretary at war in the late seventeenth century made little discernable difference to this power. Generally the division of responsibility in military affairs followed the geographical division between the two secretaryships. Naval affairs tended to be less closely regulated, with secretaries only becoming involved in relation to specific expeditions. Although the secretaries also oversaw colonial affairs, these matters were usually dealt with by standing committees of the Council rather than by the secretaries alone.

In the eighteenth century the secretaries faced intermittent challenges to the scope of their powers. From 1709 to 1726 and 1742 to 1746 a third secretaryship was created to deal with Scottish affairs as a result of the union with Scotland in 1707. A colonial secretary was appointed from 1768 to 1782, as it had become apparent that the southern secretary could not deal alone with the complexities of the growing

British Empire. But the powers of the colonial secretary were disputed by the other secretaries, and the failure of Lord George Germain over the American colonies ensured that responsibility for colonial affairs was given to the new home secretary in 1782.

An official administrative structure was slow to develop. At first, secretaries appointed their staff on a personal basis. Such staff tended to have the status of servants. After 1702 it was usual for each secretary's office to be staffed by two under-secretaries, a chief clerk and a number of clerical and messengerial officers. These appointments were often made on the basis of patronage and it was not until 1770 that the under-secretaries received a government salary. Other specialist posts existed, for example the embellisher of letters, c. 1600 to c. 1800, the translators and writers of the Government Gazette, which came under the control of one or other of the secretaries, and the law clerk who took depositions in matters affecting state policy. Other officials included the secretary for the Latin tongue, which post became a life grant and a sinecure, and interpreters, translators and decipherers.

In 1782 the modern Foreign Office was created. It was staffed by the former officials of the secretary of state for the Northern Department and the first foreign secretary was Charles James Fox. In internal organisation the Foreign Office retained the earlier division into northern and southern departments until a more elaborate structure evolved during the nineteenth century. The Home Office created from the southern department took responsibility for colonial affairs as well as Ireland, Jersey, Guernsey, Alderney, Sark and the Isle of Man until 1801. In 1801 the third secretary of state, appointed in 1794 to manage the war with France, assumed responsibility for colonial affairs as secretary of state for war and the colonies. On the outbreak of the Crimean War in 1854 a fourth secretaryship was created and the dual functions of the formerly united war and colonial department were split.

4. The State Papers Foreign: General Characteristics

The state papers held in the PRO begin at the start of the sixteenth century. Those for the reign of Henry VIII are not divided into foreign and domestic series but are mixed together. Papers relating to foreign affairs in this reign can be traced using the calendars of *Letters and Papers Foreign and Domestic, Henry VIII*, which also refer to documents not in the state papers, for example Chancery enrolments and Exchequer documents. They also refer to state papers and documents held in other institutions. (For details, see 6.1). From 1547 the papers are arranged chronologically by the monarch's reign, with separate domestic and foreign series. After 1577 the state papers foreign are divided by country and then arranged chronologically, usually with a miscellaneous group of documents at the end of each class which often include intelligence reports and intercepted material. After 1689 there are also separate collections of state papers, for example, royal letters, papers relating to foreign ministers, and a number of miscellaneous artificial classes. As the secretary had responsibilities in both foreign and domestic policy, papers relating to overseas events can be found in the state papers domestic and vice versa. A few classes of mixed domestic and foreign material occur for the later period, for example SP 8, King William's chest, 1670 to 1702, and SP 9, the Williamson collection, 1463 to 1828, which contains a good deal of varied material (see 5.11), and SP 112, which contains maps relating to England and abroad, c. 1617 to c. 1837.

Before, and to some extent after, the creation of the State Paper Office, secretaries tended to keep their papers as private possessions. In the Tudor period the state papers appear to have been looked after by clerks of the secretaries of state. In 1603, the office of Keeper of the State Papers was recognised with the appointment of Sir Thomas Lake with an annuity of £40 per annum followed by those of Levinus Munck and Thomas Wilson in 1610. Attempts made to retrieve papers after the Restoration in 1660 also suggest that many were displaced during the Civil War and Interregnum. Such irregularities in the keeping of the state papers were noted by investigations in the eighteenth century. Evidence on the keeping of these records and use of the state papers foreign can be found in SP 45, the records of the State Paper Office itself. Many early collections are to be found outside the PRO, for example in the British Library and the Bodleian Library. Others survive in private collections held in repositories throughout this country and abroad, with a particularly rich collection at Hatfield House Library which holds papers of William Cecil, first baron Burghley, and Robert Cecil, first earl of Salisbury, amongst others. Locations can be identified by consulting the National Register of Archives, which is held by the Historical Manuscripts Commission at: Quality House, Quality Court, Chancery Lane, London, WC2A 1HP.

The State Paper Office continued to exist until 1852, when an order in council transferred its papers to the custody of the master of the Rolls and the Public Record Office. Before its abolition its papers were consulted by the staff of the Foreign Office, and further attempts to catalogue the papers took place. The state papers appear to have been always arranged chronologically and were bound up in volume form in the nineteenth century. The records of the State Paper Office itself are in SP 45 from the sixteenth century to c. 1852.

The state papers foreign are the accumulated papers of the secretaries produced during the course of their duties. They consist chiefly of correspondence with representatives abroad, treaties and drafts of treaties, letters from one head of state to another, correspondence with foreign ambassadors, notes and memoranda, and material relating to military and naval policy. As there was no secretary for defence or for war at this period, war policy was part of the secretaries' general responsibilities. Although the late seventeenth century saw the appointment of the secretary at war, the two secretaries remained the higher authority for military operations and continued to issue orders, including instructions to the secretary at war and the Admiralty. As a result the state papers foreign can contain reports from the field of battle by commanders, and occasionally returns of casualties and reports from observers. Other correspondence between the secretary of state and military and naval commanders can be found in SP 87, State Papers Foreign, Military Expeditions (See section 5.13), SP 41, State Papers Military, and SP 42, State Papers Naval.

As the secretary aimed to gain as much information as possible about events on the Continent, many of the reports contain political and personal news. Information could be obtained from a variety of sources; from accredited representatives, private individuals, merchants and consuls, circulated newsletters and paid agents and informants. The consuls were initially appointed through mercantile companies trading under private charter but they often provided the first representative of the English state in a particular country and were gradually brought under government control.

4

(4)

The presentes made to the Grand Sig⁰ʳ and others the cheife of
his Comˡᵉ by the Englishe Ambassador in Constantinople the 24ᵗʰ
of Aprill 1582 —

26

Plate dubl gilt
fine clothe

iiij merrie pottes. ij fflagon bottelles. ij standinge Cuppes. 1 Basyne
and one Ewer. iiij Candelstickes. a Uarrell and a Cuppe contaynynge
1050. omnes of gilte plate at 7 ſ 4 d the onnce amounteth to — } iᶜ xlviij·00·02 348·00·02

xxxvi pirkes of fyne Clothe: viz xl piᵉˢ skarlett. xl piᵉ kleue. xl piᵉ violett in grayne xl xiij grasse greane. xl pˡ lighte greane maketh 180. yardes at sundrye pryces cometh out the one with the other after 30 ſ the yarde Amounteth to — } iiᶜ lxx·00·00 270·00·00

A uerry great and ffayer Clorke sett vpon a rocke of myne oare of siluer and other mettalles quadrate in proportion one the one quarter whearof weare to be seene men and weomen labourers some drawinge water oute of welles some diggynge of mettall some carryinge the same one wheelebarres others puryfyinge it in furnaces others washinge it hauinge all the Instrumentes belonginge to that ſpentry: one the other syde huntinge the Harte in a parke with grayhoundes and also in the forreste with houndes wherein weare Dragons lyons panthers libberdes ſarpentes Addars ſnakes grashoppers wormes and other sortes of creapinge beastes, one the other ij ſydes ouer agaynste theise weare ſhipphardes keepinge ſheepe and driuinge them to uerry fayer ffowntaynes with resterne and runinge Conduites: plowmen at tyllinge the earthe ſoldiars both horse and ffoote men in actions and ouer all theise a quadrat caſtell with a drawe bridge compassed abowte with runinge water hauinge 4. Towers replenished with ordenance and souldiars lookinge oute the windowes and walkinge one the walles and vpon the toppe of euerie Tower a uerry fayer great pearell besides uerry ffyne counterfayte emeraudes rubies diamondes and Correll wherwith in uerry many places the same was garnished and the moste parte of the worke pure siluer gilte and enameled in which Clorke ſore one quarter of an hower after it Cadde ſtroken all theise exersises hadd their mouinge in most decent and delectable order bought heare for 254 li and in Cullen wheare it was made cost 600ᵗᵉ ſtarlinge but esteamed at Constantinople worthe more then 3000 Dolleres — } iiᶜ liiij·00·00 254·00·00

More Sundry sortes of Dogges as mastis ſpanniells grayhoundes houndes: blood houndes and lyttell Dogges with their prouisione for Sea and other thinges for them Coste — } xxvj·00·00 26·00·00

more 20. peces of ffyne Hollandes some better then other coste — } vjˣˣ·00·00 120·00·00

Somma totallis of the aboue sayde presented to the Grand Sig⁰ʳ Amounteth vnto. — } m xviij·09·02 1018·09·02

chings

To the vizroy Siamo bassa

ij Liuerie pottes and ij ſtandinge Cuppes contayninge 270 onms duble gilte plate at 7 ſ 4 d the onnce amounteth to — } Cx·19·06 110·19·06

more xx peces of ffyne Cloth of the same Coullers and Clothes giuen to the Grande Sig⁰ʳ beinge 90 yardes cost one with the other at 30 ſ the yarde Amounteth to — } vˣˣ xv·00·00 135·00·00

more x peces of ffyne Hollandes at 6 li theese pece — } iijˣˣ·00·00 60·00·00

Suma lij 1324·3·8 d

iijᶜ v·19·06 305·19·06

26

SP 91/1, f 211 State Papers Foreign Russia: John Merrick to the Earl of Salisbury, 11 January 1606, reporting the death of the emperor Boris [Gudunov] and the accession of Prince Demitri, thought to be the son of Ivan the Terrible.

Before 1689 the general correspondence includes letters from foreign princes and foreign ministers residing in England. After this date there are separate classes which contain relevant information (see section 5.1).

The state papers foreign also reflect the prevailing geographical and political arrangements of the day. As a result information about specific countries and individuals may be found scattered in other classes according to the diplomatic and legal arrangements of that state. For example, SP 88, which relates to Polish affairs, also has information on Saxony for 1697 to 1764, when the elector of Saxony was also the king of Poland.

For the relations between England and Ireland, Scotland, and the Channel Islands and the Isle of Man, there are separate record classes in the state papers. Letters and papers relating to the Channel Islands (1671 to 1781) can be found in SP 47, and to the Isle of Man (1671 to 1783) in SP 48. Early material concerning the Channel Islands can be found in E 101, 17 Edward II to 6 Charles I, and includes, besides accounts, memoranda, and inventories, copies of grants and valuations. Other material relating to the Channel Islands can be found in SP 15, State Papers Domestic Addenda, Edward VI to James I (1547 to 1625), and the state papers domestic general classes. Entry books of correspondence referring to the Channel Islands between 1748 and 1760 are in SP 111.

Information about Calais during the Tudor period can be found in SP 68, State Papers Foreign, General Series, Edward VI, mainly covering 1547 to 1548, and SP 69, State Papers Foreign General Series, Mary, 1553 to 1558.

SP 58 contains transcripts of documents made in the sixteenth and seventeenth centuries of material dated 1065 to 1508 illustrating relations between England and Scotland. Other references to Scottish affairs can be found in SP 15 and SP 49 to SP 57 inclusive. The Border Papers, 1558 to 1603, are in the class SP 59, and concern events in the Scots-English border areas. The Scottish documents in E 39 include warrants, attestations, oaths of fealty, ratifications and letters of credence, 1065 to 1586. There are documents relating to diplomacy in the early Tudor period amongst the Chancery Miscellanea; C 47/24-26 contain documents relating to French possessions, c. Henry III to Henry VIII, and C 47/27-32 include some diplomatic documents relating mainly to Anglo-French-Scottish relations, c. Henry III to Henry VIII. The largely medieval Scotch rolls, C 71, continue to 7 Henry VIII (1290 to

1516), and were used for the enrolment of treaties, truces, appointments and powers of ambassadors and notes of negotiations. There is also a copy of the proposed Anglo-Scottish treaty of 1604 in PRO 30/49.

Papers covering Irish affairs can be found in SP 21, and SP 60 to SP 67 inclusive. The PRO also holds selective transcripts of material from the Carte papers, now held in the Bodleian library, which relate to Ireland, 1626 to 1668, in the class PRO 31/1. Other papers, including royal letters and other correspondence relating to Ireland for 1592 to 1615, can be found in transcript form in PRO 31/8, the Record Commissioners Transcripts, Series II. The originals of these records were destroyed in 1922 in the fire at the Four Courts in Dublin, where the Irish archives were kept. Other documents concerning Irish affairs can be found amongst the Shaftesbury papers, PRO 30/24, for 1641 to 1700. Later records relating to Ireland are spread through a number of classes. The easiest way to approach them is to consult a guide by Alice Prochaska entitled *Irish History from 1700: A Guide to Sources in the Public Record Office* (British Records Association, 1986).

The main languages of diplomacy were Latin, French and Italian during this period, and documents in the state papers foreign are often in these languages, occasionally with translations. In general there are always papers in the language of the country concerned within the state paper classes arranged by state or region, and sometimes a variety of languages can be found. A reading knowledge of French, German, Italian or Latin is a great advantage in using these documents, as is some practice in reading sixteenth and seventeenth century secretary hand and italic script.

Use of cipher was frequent from the fifteenth century and examples are scattered throughout the state papers. These are not necessarily deciphered, and recourse may be needed to other documents in state paper classes or in documents held elsewhere to find the key (see section 5.8 for a more detailed description).

For a list of state paper classes by broad geographical area from 1577 see appendix 20.1.

5. Special state paper classes

There are also state paper classes which are concerned with a specific type of record, for example maps (SP 112), ciphers (SP 106), or intercepted despatches (SP 107). However, this does not mean that such material is necessarily confined to that class alone and it is possible to find all types of state paper documents in the general foreign and domestic series.

5.1 Records of foreign ministers in England

Letters, memorials, and other documents of ministers accredited to the court of St James can be found in SP 100, for the period 1684 to 1780. The documents are arranged chronologically by country. Before 1684 they are available in the country and chronological classes of the state papers foreign. Papers of foreign diplomats may also occur in these classes after this date. SP 100 also contains some miscellaneous correspondence concerning diplomatic immunity, 1719 to 1774. Further material can be found in the Foreign Entry Books in SP 104 (see section 5.6) which contains correspondence with ambassadors in England from the following countries in a series of secretaries' letterbooks: Denmark (1715-26), France (1713-19), the German Empire (1714), German States (1714-28), Holland (1715, 1725-1726 and 1713-1746), Italy (1713-1746), Portugal (1713-1745), Prussia (1715-1726), Russia (1714-1720), Spain (1713-1726), and Sweden (1714-27). Some miscellaneous letterbooks concerning the privileges of foreign ministers and their servants, 1710 to 1782, are also in SP 104.

5.2 Newsletters

Newsletters were unsigned, handwritten accounts of events in a particular country which appear to have been circulated in the individual country concerned, and copies of which found their way into the hands of officials in other states who used them for intelligence purposes. The main PRO class for these records is SP 101, which includes newsletters from 1565 to 1763. This class includes copies of foreign gazettes and news-sheets produced in other countries which were intercepted and which provide comments on how British policy was perceived overseas. They are especially numerous for the reigns of Charles II and James II. This class also includes copies of despatches sent from Dutch agents abroad to the Hague, 1622, 1664 to 1668, and 1711 to 1715, as well as a more general series of news from

France, Switzerland and the Low Countries collected at the Hague, 1702 to 1706, 1710 to 1712 and 1718 to 1726.

5.3 Royal Letters

The class SP 102, covering c. 1564 to c. 1780, includes original letters and copies of letters from foreign royalty and heads of state and the drafts of British replies. They are mostly formal exchanges of courtesies and are arranged by country and then chronologically. There are letters from the rulers of: the Barbary States; China; Denmark; Flanders; France; German States; Holland; the Holy Roman Empire; the Ottoman Empire; Poland; Persia; Portugal; Russia; Senegal; Spain; Sweden; Switzerland; Tuscany; Venice; Prussia; Savoy; and the two Sicilies. There are manuscript calendars, with tables of contents by country, in IND 1/6838-6842 and IND 1/6843-6845. These refer to an earlier arrangement and are not keyed to the present organisation of the documents, apart for the reign of Queen Anne. SP 104 and FO 90 also contain entry books of letters from British sovereigns to foreign heads of state. Later royal letters (1781 to 1930) can be found amongst the records of the Foreign Office in FO 95; see section 16.3.

5.4 Treaty Papers

SP 103 includes papers of ministers and plenipotentiaries involved in the negotiation and drafting of treaties involving England and the United Kingdom and others from 1577 to 1780. The papers are arranged by country and then chronologically. There are also papers relating to treaties among the state papers domestic, for example letters and papers produced by negotiators at the peace of Ryswick, 1697, can be found in SP 8/17 and there are treaty notes 1671 to 1674 and 1676 in SP 29/377-387 inclusive. There are also treaty papers in the Sir Joseph Williamson and Sir Leoline Jenkins collections which can be found in SP 105. For a general description of treaties and treaty papers see section 15.1.

Letterbooks of the secretaries of state regarding peace negotiations in the early eighteenth century are in SP 105. Peace negotiations at Utrecht, 1711 to 1714, are covered in SP 105/258-264 and SP 105/271-280. Separate entry books for dealings with France were kept between 1711 and 1714 (SP 105/265-268) and with Spain for the same period (SP 105/269-270). There is also an entry book of treaties and treaty papers for the German states and the Grand Alliance, 1689 to 1696, in SP 105/83 (George Stepney letterbooks).

Extract of the Treaty between the Emperor, Great Britain and the States General.
Hague 7.th Sept.r 1701.

Whereas upon the Death of Charles the Second, King of Spain the Emperor has asserted his Pretensions to that Monarchy in his most august Family, and whereas the French King has possessed himself of the said Monarchy for the Duke of Anjou, as also of the Spanish Low Countrys & the Dutchy of Milan by which the Emperor will lose his Fiefs in Italy, the States their Barrier, & England it's Commerce; Therefore the abovenamed Powers have agreed upon the following Articles.

1.   A perpetual Amity between the Contracting Powers.

2.   To procure a just and reasonable Satisfaction to the Emperor for his Pretensions to the Succession of Spain & a sufficient Security to Great Britain & the States for their several Kingdoms, Possessions and Commerce;

3.

SP 103/104   Treaty Papers: first page of an abstract of the Grand Alliance of Britain, the Empire and Holland of 1701, formed to prevent the union of the Spanish Empire with France during the Spanish succession crisis, dated 7 September 1701, N S.

5.5 Treaties

The class SP 108 contains protocols of treaties with ratifications, abstracts, certified copies, full powers, conventions, renewals of capitulations and subsidiary documents from 1579 to 1780. These records are also arranged by country and then chronologically. Treaties relating to royal marriages are arranged separately within the class and cover the date range 1579 to 1766. There are entry books of treaties, 1639 to 1780, in FO 95. For overlaps with FO classes, see section 20.2.

5.6 Entry Books

SP 104, the State Papers Foreign Entry Books, 1571 to 1783, contains a set of official out-letter books with correspondence from the secretary of state to representatives abroad. These books are not complete, and are arranged by country rather than by secretary of state. There are also some précis books, summarising in-coming and out-going correspondence, as well as draft minutes of the Committee of Foreign Affairs, 1667 to 1678. This class also contains registers of instructions given to special diplomatic missions and of allowances paid to those involved, 1671 to 1687 and 1760 to 1770, an entry book of letters to the Board of Trade (covering 1763-1767), and entry books of letters from British monarchs to foreign heads of state, c. 1603 to c. 1723.

Other draft letter books of the Northern Department, 1726 to 1744, and précis books of correspondence of both departments, 1756 to 1775, can be found in SP 109, State Papers Foreign, Various. This class also contains some miscellaneous correspondence, including that of the commissioners appointed for the inspection of the accounts of the allied army in Spain, Portugal and Italy during 1708 to 1713. There are also records of negotiations with the United Provinces in 1672, accounts of ambassadors and envoys, 1689 to 1727 and 1749, lists of ministers and consuls in the service of the Northern Department and Southern Department, and economic reports on France (1759-1772), Sardinia (1760), Spain (1760), Austria (1768) and Prussia (army only, 1773), presumably gathered during the Seven Years War.

The State Papers Foreign, Supplementary in SP 110 also include letter books and correspondence of British envoys to Denmark, (1770-1780), France (1768-1770), the Ottoman Empire, (1684-1691 and 1766-1769), Spain (1735-1770), Germany, Bavaria, the Imperial Diet and Prussia, (1745-1800). Much of SP 110 consists of material relating to the consulate at Aleppo, mainly the records of factors based there (see sections 5.7 and 5.12). There is also one volume for the consulate general and British factory in Portugal and two volumes of private correspondence concerning trade and shipping movements from Santa Cruz de la Mar Pequena, Morocco. SP 110 also contains Northern Department letter books for 1719, 1721 to 1745, 1768, 1760 to 1782, and 1799 to 1800.

There are also a number of miscellaneous entry books in the domestic state paper classes which refer to foreign affairs. For example, SP 44/1 contains domestic and foreign letters of the secretaries of state, 1661 to 1662, SP 44/64 letters from the Southern Department 1680 to 1684, and SP 44/68 includes those from the Northern Department, 1680 to 1683.

Occasionally diplomatic entry books may be found amongst the state papers foreign classes arranged by reign and by country; one of the earliest is that of Sir John Mason as ambassador to France (c. 1550 to 1551) in SP 68/9A. Other entry books for the late eighteenth century are in FO 95.

SP 104/262, f 207 State Papers Foreign Entry Books: copy of Charles James Fox's circular to the Northern Courts announcing his appointment as Foreign Secretary, dated 2 April 1783.

Additionall Instructions for Our Trusty and Welbeloved Sir Henry Goodrick Knt. Our Envoy Extraordinary to the Catholique King

Besides the former Instructions given you, Wee have thought fitt to adde these following. That you endeavour with your utmost Addresse to possesse that Court of Our reall desires and endeavours for the Prosperity of that Cronne, & particularly the Spanish Netherlands, in whose preservation Wee take Our self equally concerned as in Our owne Territorys. You shall putt them in mind with what earnestnesse Wee prest the French King whare consented to more advantageous Conditions then those it was at last Concluded on. That when Wee saw that could not be obtained with what great Charge Wee voyed an Army and your self being an Officer in it can tell them know how considerable a part of it was transported over for the preservation of the ~~Spanish Netherlands~~ those Countrys. how they were upon their march after the Batail of Mons & had probably within few dayes been in open action had not the News of the peace ~~put a stop~~ concluded betwixt that King and the States putt a stop to all Hostlities.

That since his Catholique Maty judged it his interest to make the Peace, Wee have continually used Our interest with the most Christian King for his observing the Articles of it, and there is nothing Wee lay more to heart then how to secure what is left of those Countrys, And that Wee shall take the best measures Wee can in Conjunction with those that are Our ~~best~~ joynt Friends here both to secure it.

Given at Our Court at Whitehall the 10th day of June 1679 in the one and Thirtieth year of Our Reigne

C. R.

By his Maty Command
H. C.

48

SP 104/239, f 48   State Papers Foreign Entry Books: additional instructions from King Charles II to Sir Henry Goodrick as envoy extraordinary to Spain, 10 June 1679.

5.7 Archives of British Legations

The State Papers Foreign, Archives of British Legations, in SP 105, include letter books, diaries, drafts and correspondence between the secretaries and embassies and legations abroad from 1568 to c. 1796. Material relating to the Levant Company covers 1606 to 1866, and is listed separately within the class. Archives of legations may also be found in SP 109, State Papers, Various. This class contains lists of English ambassadors, consuls and envoys under the authority of the Northern and Southern Departments, 1755 to 1766, and accounts of the same, 1689 to 1749. Archives of British legations in Denmark (1770-1780), Germany (the Holy Roman Empire, Bavaria, and Imperial Diet, 1745-1800), Prussia (1719, 1721-1722, 1777-1782), the Levant Company (mainly the station at Aleppo, 1600-1825), Spain (1735-1770) and the Ottoman Empire (1684-1691, 1766-1769), can also be found in SP 110, State Papers Supplementary. These records can be used to supplement the general correspondence and are the precursors of the Foreign Office consular material.

Correspondence with consuls can also be found amongst the country classes of the state papers foreign.

SP 105/102   Archives of British legations: copy of instructions to
Edward Kirkham, Consul at Aleppo, 1622.

5.8 Ciphers

A collection of official ciphers with some deciphers from the reign of Elizabeth I to George III is in the class SP 106. The documents are arranged chronologically. Of particular interest is SP 106/67 which contains draft and decoded correspondence to and from Joseph Ewart, envoy extraordinary to Brandenburg-Prussia 1787 to 1788, and from Charles Whitworth, envoy extraordinary to Russia, 1789 to 1791. Piece SP 106/10 includes some royalist intercepted letters from the civil war period. Samples of these documents, including the royalist material, are described more fully in Sheila R Richards, ed. *Secret Writing in the Public Records, Henry VIII to George III*, (HMSO, 1974).

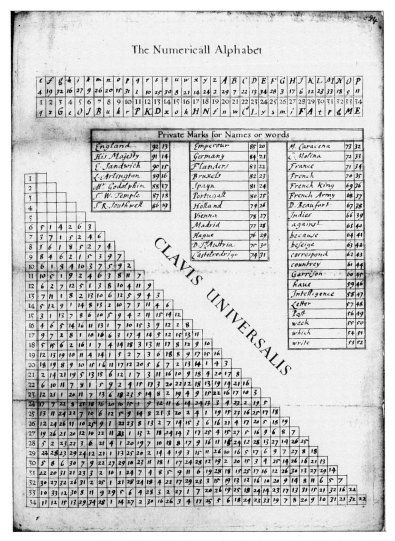

SP 106/6   Cipher made for the Earl of Sandwich, 9 October 1667.

5.9 Intercepted Despatches

The State Papers Confidential, 1716 to 1766, in SP 107 contain a collection of copies, translations and extracts from the correspondence of foreign ministers resident in England. This correspondence was usually intercepted before delivery by the Post Office in London and deciphered and copied in the 'Secret Office' maintained by the secretaries of state until its abolition in 1844-1847. Other intercepted material is often included in the state papers foreign under individual countries, usually listed in a separate section at the end of the list of papers relating to a particular country. Copies of intercepts might be sent outwards to representatives if considered necessary. Some later intercepts can be found in FO 83, FO 95 and FO 360. Papers relating to the later history of the Secret Office can be found in HD 3, records of the expenditure of the Secret Service by the Undersecretary at the Foreign Office.

SP 107/62   Intercepted despatches: intercepted letter of the Baron de Honberg to the Conte de Brühl, with news of Prince Charles Edward Stuart's movements on the continent, and expected landing in Scotland, 30 July 1745, O S.

5.10 Gazettes and Pamphlets

There are a number of state paper classes which contain printed material, such as newspapers, gazettes, pamphlets, broadsides, and proclamations. Most of this material was at one point extracted from the state papers and held in the PRO library, and it has since proved impossible to reconstitute the original arrangement. These are now arranged in classes covering general topics and specific countries as follows: Denmark, 1641 to 1679, (SP 115); Holy Roman Empire, 1663 to [1791], (SP 118); United Provinces, 1664 to 1784, (SP 119); Italian States, 1663 to 1679, (SP 120); Spanish Netherlands, 1666 to 1688, (SP 121, in French, Spanish and Flemish); Poland, 1637 to 1704, (SP 122, in Polish, German, and Latin); Russia, [1718], (SP 124); Sweden, [1598] to 1677, (SP 126) and Switzerland, 1666, 1673 and 1675 (SP 127, in Dutch, Italian and French). The class SP 116 refers to England, 1591 to 1780, but contains material relating to the conduct of diplomacy and military and naval events. The class SP 128 under the general heading 'outside Europe' is as yet unavailable as are some other classes of gazettes which are still in the process of arrangement and listing, but which should be available shortly. These include SP 117 (France), SP 123 (Portugal), and SP 125 (Spain). Other printed material may exist randomly in the state paper classes arranged by state.

5.11 State papers miscellaneous (Williamson Collection)

The class SP 9 contains both foreign and domestic material, c. 1463 to 1828, the basis of which was formed from the papers of the late seventeenth-century diplomat and secretary of state Sir Joseph Williamson which were left to the State Paper Office. Other papers were added later to the collection. Besides domestic papers and pamphlets, it includes a selection of foreign diplomatic reports from various countries of varying dates, particularly Spain, France, Germany and the Netherlands, and many reports on papal diplomacy and politics. There are also accounts of foreign envoys, notes on treaties, and extracts from a variety of sources concerning diplomatic precedence, privilege, and title in the seventeenth and eighteenth centuries. There are also formularies, treatises on diplomacy and ambassadors, copies of treaties, tracts on the gathering of intelligence and a list of the governors of the plantations, c. 1675 (SP 9/244A). Amongst the printed material are alphabetical indexes of diplomatic representatives from the sixteenth to the eighteenth centuries. These include printed nineteenth century indexes to English representatives abroad, lists of diplomats exchanged between England and the Spanish Netherlands, 1558 to 1660, England and the Spanish-Austrian Netherlands, 1660 to 1780, and England and Germany, 1547 to 1666, (SP 9/256-257, 260-261, 263).

5.12 Records of the Levant Company

The state papers also include many papers of the Levant Company. These can be found in a number of classes. SP 105 contains books and papers, dated 1606 to 1866, and a copy of the company's charter of 1605. These records mainly consist of order and letter books for inward and outward correspondence, miscellaneous correspondence, minute books, and various registers from the chancery at Constantinople concerning accounts, petitions, acts and trade impositions. SP 110 contains records of the consulate of Aleppo, which was maintained by the Levant Company, for the period 1634 to 1871. Some of the later records are those of the consulate when under Foreign Office control. SP 110/70 is a register of marriages, baptisms and burials kept by the chaplain of the factory in Aleppo, 1756 to 1800, but most of the class consists of minute books, company registers (which can include references to wills and inventories) and letter books. There is also some correspondence about the Levant Company in FO 261, which includes a letter book of Sir Robert Ainslie to British consuls and ministers abroad, 1776 to 1778. Another letter book of Ainslie can be found under the reference PRO 30/26/72, covering 1776 to 1793. SP 105 also includes the journal of Sir Thomas Roe's embassy to the Ottoman Empire, 1622 to 1625. The main group of papers which includes correspondence between the secretary of state and the company, can be found in SP 97, covering 1577 to 1779. Included are registers, court books, ledgers, material relating to impositions, and transcripts of concessions and tariffs. (Charters for the incorporation of companies, including the East India Company, are enrolled on the Patent rolls, C66).

The PRO does not contain the papers of the Russia Company. Most of the Company's archives were destroyed in the Great Fire of London, but a few papers survive amongst the state papers Russia in SP 91.

5.13 State Papers Military Expeditions

Correspondence of the secretaries of state with military commanders in the field, 1695 to 1763, can be found in SP 87. Papers produced in the course of diplomatic negotiations are also sometimes included. The major campaigns referred to include those of the war of the Spanish succession (1702-1713), the war of the Austrian succession (1740-1748) and the Seven Years War (1756-1763).

6. Means of Reference to the State Papers Foreign

6.1 Calendars

Summaries of many state papers are available in printed published form. Some of the most useful are listed below.

For the period 1509 to 1547, refer to:
Letters and Papers, Foreign and Domestic, Henry VIII (HMSO, 1864-1932). 21 volumes and 2 volumes of addenda.
Keys to these calendars are available in the Round Room at Chancery Lane. The calendars also refer to other documents which are not state papers and are held in other classes or elsewhere.

For the period 1547 to 1589, refer to:
Calendar of State Papers Foreign, Edward VI, 1547-1553, 1 volume (HMSO, 1861)
Calendar of State Papers Foreign, Mary, 1553-1558, 1 volume (HMSO, 1861)
Calendar of State Papers Foreign, Elizabeth, 1558-1589, 23 volumes (HMSO, 1863-1950)
List and Analysis of State Papers Foreign, Elizabeth, 1589-1595, 6 volumes (HMSO, 1964-1993.)

For Anglo-Scottish relations, refer to:
Calendar of State Papers relating to Scotland and Mary, Queen of Scots, 1547-1603, preserved in the Public Record Office, the British Museum, and elsewhere in England, 13 volumes (HMSO, 1898-1969)
Calendar of Letters and Papers relating to the Affairs of the Borders of England and Scotland, 1560-1603, 2 volumes (HMSO, 1894, 1896)

6.2 Lists

After 1577 there are basic class lists for all state papers foreign. The following classes have more detailed lists or are semi-calendared in part. The third column refers to the date range covered by the expanded list.

SP 75	Denmark	1585-1659
SP 77	Flanders	1589-1659
SP 78	France	1577-1589, 1589-1659, (calendars only, see above) 1699-1714, 1727-1779*
SP 79	Genoa	1584-1669
SP 80	German Empire	1591-1659, 1661-1700
SP 81	German States	1589-1661
SP 82	Hamburg, Hanse Towns	[1588]-1659, 1660-1675
SP 84	Holland	[c. 1560]-1665
SP 85	Italian States and Rome	1544-1664, 1690-1773
SP 88	Poland	1586-1661
SP 89	Portugal	1590-1660, 1661-1765, 1724-1780, 1661-1780. The latter is an index of names and subjects.
SP 90	Prussia	1698-1719
SP 91	Russia	1589-1655, 1704-1743
SP 102	Royal letters, Russia	1570-1682
SP 92	Sardinia and Savoy	1579-1670
SP 93	Sicily, Naples	1584-1675, 1584-1702, The latter is a calendar in Italian, unindexed.
SP 94	Spain	1578-1659
SP 95	Sweden	[1570]-1660

SP 96	Switzerland	[1582]-1660
SP 97	Turkey	1579-1662
SP 98	Tuscany	1582-1664
SP 99	Venice	1559-1686
SP 105	Archives of Legations abroad	1686-1697, selected archives, English lega-tions.

*The state papers for France were partially registered for 1761-1768; this register is held under the reference FO 802/223 at Kew.

The IND 1 class of original indexes includes many volumes referring to the state papers foreign (IND 1/6854-6864, 6872-6906). The indexes provide useful information on the previous arrangement of the documents, but they do not correspond to the present references for the state paper classes.

6.3 Other Calendars (Sources held abroad)

Spain

Letters, Despatches and State Papers, relating to the Negotiations between England and Spain, preserved in the Archives at Vienna, Brussels, Simancas and Elsewhere, 1485 to 1558, 13 volumes (HMSO, 1862-1954).
Letters and State Papers relating to English Affairs, preserved in the Archives of Simancas, 1558-1603, 4 volumes (HMSO,1892-1899).

Italy

Entries in the Papal Registers relating to Great Britain and Ireland, 1198-1492, 14 volumes (HMSO, 1894-1961).
State Papers, relating to English Affairs, in the Vatican Archives and Library, 1558-1578, 2 volumes (HMSO, 1916 and 1926)
State Papers and Manuscripts relating to English Affairs, existing in the Archives and Collections of Venice, and in other libraries of Northern Italy, 1202-1674, 38 volumes (HMSO, 1864-1947).
State Papers and Manuscripts existing in the Archives Collection of Milan, 1359-1618, 1 volume (HMSO, 1913).

7. Other Early Modern Sources

Audit Office

The class AO 1, held at Kew, includes references to agents employed abroad for special purposes 1563 to 1819, and expenditure on army campaigns, as well as the accounts for ambassadors' services in Denmark, France and Germany, 1620 to 1629. There are also accounts of ambassadors, 1620 to 1827, which are arranged by name, but do not cover the above date range comprehensively. They also refer to repairs to residencies, subsidies and presents to foreign rulers and include some military accounts.

Carew Papers

Part of the Carew papers can be found in PRO 30/5, c. 1528 to 1645. These papers were collected by Thomas Carew (1702-1766) and contain many unique documents relating to the work of the secretaries of state. The manuscripts in the PRO include a letter book of Cardinal Wolsey which contains transcripts of letters to English diplomats in the 1520s (PRO 30/5/1).

Lowndes Papers, Charles I to 1886

In T 48 there are secret service accounts for the late seventeenth century, including the payments and receipts of Henry Guy and William Lowndes, the secretary to the Treasury, c. 1679 to 1710. These consist mainly of original accounts and copy books. Some of the early papers concern Scottish, Irish and military and naval affairs and the provision of newsletters from the continent. These documents can only be consulted at Kew.

8. Papers of Secretaries of State and Diplomats: 1500-1782

Further details of the locations of the papers of secretaries of state and diplomats held in the PRO and elsewhere can be found in the following works:

Bell, G M, *A Handlist of British Diplomatic Representatives 1509-1688* (Royal Historical Society, 1990).

Horn, D B, *British Diplomatic Representatives 1689-1789* Camden Society 3rd Series, volume XLVI (London, 1932).

The National Register of Archives held by the Royal Commission on Historical Manuscripts, Quality House, Quality Court, Chancery Lane WC2A 1HP should also be consulted for the location of private papers.

The following papers of secretaries of state and diplomats can be found in the PRO. Please note that this list does not include all 'papers' of diplomats which appear in the general classes of state papers foreign.

Aldworth, Richard Neville, (afterwards Richard Neville Neville) as under-secretary of state, 1744 to 1752, and secretary to the embassy in Paris, 1762 to 1763 (PRO 30/50/33-46, 48-60, Neville and Aldworth papers). Pieces PRO 30/50/59-69 contain various semi-official and private letters, dated 1710, 1747 to 1757, and 1750 to 1799. See also SP 78 and PRO 30/47.

Bentinck, William, duke of Portland, letter book 1698 (SP 105/26).

Burrish, Onslow, letter books and papers 1742 to 1746 (SP 105/22-25); 1741 to 1757 (SP 110/6); 1747 to 1758 (SP 105/33-38).

Carleton, Sir Dudley, letter books 1616 to 1619, 1612 to 1613 (SP 105/94-96, 106).

Chatham papers - See Pitt, William

Cooper, Charles Purton, 1793 to 1873 (PRO 30/41, Cooper collection). This class includes part of a private collection of original manuscripts, entry books and transcripts, c. 1152 to 1720. It also contains documents on French diplomatic relations, including letters and entry books of French diplomats covering the seventeenth and eighteenth centuries, and transcripts of medieval documents in the French archives relating to England.

Crowe, Sir Sackville, letter book, 1638 to 1643 (SP 105/103).

Eden, Morton, letter books, 1780 to 1789 (SP 105/3-4), 1776 to 1780 (SP 105/43-44).

Eden, William, letter books, 1774 to 1777 (SP 105/41).

Egremont, earl of, see Wyndham, Charles

Elliot, Hugh, letter books, 1774 to 1776 and 1774 to 1781 (SP 105/40-42, and SP 110/9).

Goodricke, Sir John, letter books, 1760 to 1762 (SP 105/1).

Heathcote, Ralph, letter books, 1778 to 1781 (SP 105/45-46).

Herbert Edward, Lord Herbert of Cherbury, ambassador to France, 1619 to 1624 (PRO 30/53/1-6 inclusive, Powis papers), miscellaneous correspondence.

Jenkins, Sir Leoline, letter books, 1673 to 1679, 1697 (SP 105/233-257).

Lisle, see Plantagenet, Arthur

Mann, Sir Horace, letter books, 1737 to 1786, 1783 to 1786 (SP 105/281-303, 308-321, 331).

de Mesmes, Jean Antoine, Comte D'Avaux, 1614 to 1709 (FO 95). Correspondence, papers, and entry books relating to various missions to Venice, Holland, Sweden and Ireland, as well as the Nimeguen negotiations.

Murray, John, letter book, 1768 to 1775 (SP 105/104)

Neville, Sir Henry (Neville and Aldworth papers, PRO 30/50/1-8, 70). Letters and papers of Sir Henry Neville, 1570 to 1609, with papers while ambassador at Paris, 1598 to 1600.

Pitt, William, the Elder, earl of Chatham (PRO 30/8, FO 90, FO 95, FO 366). See also the Hoare (Pitt) papers 1667 to 1946 in PRO 30/70 for other correspondence of the Pitt family.

Plantagenet, Arthur, Lord Lisle, deputy of Calais, 1533 to 1540 (SP 3). Correspondence when deputy of Calais. Mainly letters to Lady Lisle and unsigned papers.

Portland, duke of - see Bentinck, William

Prior, Matthew, letter book, 1712 to 1715 (SP 105/27-29). Includes correspondence relating to Ireland, 1641 to 1700, and to America and the colonies.

Roe, Sir Thomas, letter book, 1622 to 1625 (SP 105/102).

Southwell, Sir Robert, letter book, 1680 (SP 105/49).

Stepney, George, letter books, 1691 to 1692, 1694 to 1697, 1698 to 1699, 1701 to 1707 (SP 105/50-89).

Trevor, John, letter books, 1780 to 1784 (SP 105/47).

Walpole, Robert, correspondence, 1768 to 1770 (SP 110/5).

Walsingham, Sir Francis, secretary of state 1573 to 1590 (PRO 30/5, Carew Papers). Contains an entry book of letters to officials in Ireland, 1578 to 1579, as well as a general diary, 1570 to 1583.

Williamson, Sir Joseph, letter books, 1673 to 1674 (SP 105/219-232).

Wotton, Sir Henry, letter book, 1609 to 1610 (SP 105/105).

Wriothesley, Sir Thomas (SP 7). One volume of letters to Wriothesley, 1536 to 1540.

Wyndham, Charles, 2nd earl Egremont, secretary of state, Southern Department, 1761 to 1763 (PRO 30/47). Papers and correspondence relating to the peace of Paris, miscellaneous letters and treaty papers, 1745, 1754, and 1756 to 1763, and material relating to the colonies and America, 1703 to 1763.

Wyndham, W F, letter books, 1788 to 1796, 1795 to 1796 (SP105/306-307, 322).

9. Transcripts of Documents Held Abroad

The PRO contains a number of deposits of transcriptions of documents, largely made in the course of production of calendars (see sections 6.1). These transcriptions are of British material and of documents held abroad. While many of the foreign documents refer to events in the individual country concerned, diplomatic reports and documents relating specifically to Britain can be found in them. The Venetian transcripts are particularly useful in this respect.

Milan Archives:

PRO 31/2, 1425 to 1786. Compiled for the *Calendar of state papers and manuscripts existing in the Archives and Collections of Milan*, volume I.

Paris Archives:

Baschet's transcripts, PRO 31/3, 1504 to 1714, taken from documents in the French National Archives in Paris relating to affairs in England and Ireland.
Crisp's transcripts, PRO 31/4, 1624 to 1625. Transcripts of letters and acts relating to the marriage of Charles I and Henrietta Maria of France.
Other transcripts, including some from the royal archives, can be found in PRO 31/8, c. 1162 to c. 1572.

Rome Archives

PRO 31/9 series 1, 1066 to c.1815
PRO 31/10 series 2, c.1200 to James I

Spanish Archives

PRO 31/11 series 1, 1485 to 1555
PRO 31/12 series 2, 1594 to 1672 (Gondomar Mss.)

Stockholm Archives

 PRO 31/13, 1550 to 1791
See also *Deputy Keeper's report XLIII*, appendix II.

Venetian Archives

PRO 31/14, 1202 to 1797. Transcriptions of despatches, diaries, reports of Venetian ambassadors, and newsletters. See also *Letters and Papers, Foreign and Domestic of Henry VIII* and *Calendars of State Papers Venetian*. Despatches from Venetian ambassadors in England can also be found in PRO 31/14/1-55, covering 1505 to 1597.

Venetian Manuscripts

PRO 30/25, 1224 to 1877. Collection of manuscripts and printed pamphlets acquired by Rawdon Brown, the editor of the *Calendar of State Papers Venetian*. See also *Deputy Keeper's report XLVI*, appendix II.

Vienna Archives

PRO 31/18, 1513 to 1543. Material collected for a projected calendar of state papers.

Transcripts of other foreign documents concerning diplomatic relations with Britain can be found in PRO 31/8 for: Saxony (1504 to 1688); Prussia (fourteenth to seventeenth centuries); Germany (c. 1340 to 1566) and Portugal (c. 1338 to 1689).

10. The Foreign Office and the Foreign Secretary

On 27 March 1782 Charles James Fox was appointed secretary of state for foreign affairs. Domestic and foreign policy was now divided between two secretaries of state with defined responsibilities. The foreign secretary was assisted by a permanent body of officials in the Foreign Office itself and by a separate diplomatic and consular service abroad. At first the Foreign Office maintained the older division between northern and southern affairs which reflected the geographical division of foreign duties between the secretaries of state before 1782. In the course of the nineteenth century, with an ever-increasing workload and greater complexity in foreign affairs, the numbers of departments grew. On the whole these political departments were organised on a geographical basis, although there were functional departments, for example the Chief Clerk's Department and the Slave Trade Department. In the late twentieth century these functional or specialist sections have tended to become more common as examination of the more recent editions of the *Diplomatic List* shows.

The foreign secretary was, and is, responsible for the conduct of foreign policy on a day to day basis, and for presentation of policy to the Cabinet and to Parliament. Some prime ministers, for example the duke of Wellington, the third marquess of Salisbury and Ramsay MacDonald, combined the offices of foreign secretary and prime minister, while others, most notably Lloyd George, Neville Chamberlain and Churchill, intervened personally in the conduct of diplomacy. In the post Second World War period it has become increasingly common for the foreign secretary to be personally involved in international negotiations. The Foreign Office, or Foreign Department as it was originally known, conducts all correspondence with foreign states, negotiates with ministers and ambassadors, and corresponds with other government departments where necessary.

During the nineteenth century the Foreign Office developed a professionally organised structure, as did the Diplomatic Service abroad. Under the impact of home civil service reform, examinations for entrance to the Foreign Office and Diplomatic Service were instituted in 1856, the two entrance tests becoming identical in 1892. But patronage, nomination by the foreign secretary and the 'property qualification' of £400 per annum ensured a largely aristocratic personnel up to 1919. The Foreign

Office clerks were, at the start of the nineteenth century, employed mainly on routine copying. They did not have policy tasks and it was considered improper for unelected officials to have such influence on national policy. By the turn of the century, however, this situation had changed. Under the impact of the reforms of Sir Edward Grey and Sir Eyre Crowe, officials now minuted and prepared papers and commented on despatches. In this respect the records of the Foreign Office reflect this evolution; early papers can contain much semi-personal correspondence between the secretary of state and diplomats abroad, while the papers of the early twentieth century have many more formal documents produced by diplomats and officials.

The Foreign Office and agencies responsible for other aspects of policy overseas have undergone a gradual amalgamation in the twentieth century. At the present date, all the main agencies dealing with the conduct of British relations abroad have been incorporated into a unified Foreign and Commonwealth Office, which was established in 1968. With the narrowing of British involvement in the administration of colonial and Commonwealth territory most activities relating to the conduct of British policy overseas are now conducted through this office.

The modern twentieth century records of the Foreign Office reflect the growth in the complexity of foreign affairs, the increase in the number of states to which Britain has accredited representatives and the expansion in the numbers of international organisations in which Britain plays a part. The documents also show the effects of the communications revolution: increased use of telegraphs, despatches arriving more quickly and in greater numbers, typewritten accounts, and, in the twentieth century, notes of telephone conversations. The records also illustrate the results of the impact of the revolution in international communication and the media in an organisational sense, as more departments have been formed to deal with different aspects of publicity and information policy, particularly after the Second World War.

The records of the Foreign Office also vastly outnumber those records produced during the course of diplomacy in the early modern period, c. 1500 to 1800. With the use of modern filing and organisational systems, which have evolved to meet the need of imposing order on large accretions of documents, more sophisticated indexing and referencing systems evolved. These contemporary systems can now be used in roughly the same manner as by the originators to locate particular files or subjects. Guidance in using these systems is provided in chapter 18.

11. The Diplomatic and Consular Services

The Diplomatic Service had its earliest origins in the use of household officers and servants by medieval monarchs. It did not have an ordered structure until the early nineteenth century. In 1785 there were twenty-one accredited representatives abroad, of which only three ranked as ambassadorial posts (Paris, Constantinople and Madrid). Real expansion in the service came only after the Napoleonic Wars, with the elaboration of diplomatic ranks, the decline of the family embassy and the depoliticisation of personnel, with the exception of the parliamentary under secretary of state. By 1816 the more junior embassy officials were formally called attachés, and by 1862 a regular structure had been established, with the classification of officials below the rank of ambassador or head of legation into first, second and third secretaries, attachés and keepers of archives.

The Diplomatic Service was amalgamated with the Foreign Office in 1918 to form a unified organisation. Before this date it had become more common for members of the Foreign Office to be appointed to diplomatic posts abroad and members of the Diplomatic Service to be posted to London. In 1943 the Foreign and Diplomatic Services underwent a further amalgamation, this time with the Consular Service and the Commercial Diplomatic Service which had been established in 1920 under the Department of Overseas Trade to oversee international trading relations. In 1965 the Foreign Service was amalgamated with the Commonwealth Service to form a united Colonial and Diplomatic Service.

In the twentieth century it has become increasingly common for specialists to be appointed to foreign missions. Military and naval attachés made their appearance in the latter half of the nineteenth century, as did the first commercial attaché, who was appointed in 1880. Air attachés made their appearance after 1918. This tendency has continued and there may now be specialised advisers for labour, social, cultural or economic affairs. Their reports can be found amongst the general correspondence of the Foreign Office in FO 371, in FO 366 and sometimes in the embassy and consular correspondence for the country concerned, as well as in the records of other related departments.

The Consular Service has had a similarly long history from medieval times. Several distinct branches developed as the representatives of the great trading companies were brought under governmental appointment and control. At the beginning of the twentieth century these were the General Consular Service, which had been reorganised in 1903; the Levant Service, which had taken over the responsibilities of the Levant Company after its dissolution in 1825, and the Far Eastern Service (comprising the China, Japan and Siam services, which also had representatives in other areas of the east). In 1919, after considerable opposition from the Board of Trade, a Commercial Diplomatic Service was established. These services had their own traditions and specialised training. In 1936 the three services, apart from the Commercial Diplomatic Service, were amalgamated.

A formal department to deal with consular affairs was created in the Foreign Office only in 1825. During the nineteenth century consular affairs were often combined with commercial, slave trade or African policy in a succession of political departments, the records of which are scattered through individual country classes before 1906 and in the general correspondence classes, mainly FO 83 and FO 95.

The records of the consulates and embassies and their staff form a separate set of classes amongst what are generally termed the Foreign Office records. Embassy and consular records were created within the country to which the representatives were accredited. The correspondence of the officials of the Foreign Office in London with these representatives are part of the central records of the Office, and for that reason can be found amongst the general correspondence classes.

Other services dealing with overseas policy were the Colonial Service and the India Service. Records relating to the work of the Colonial Service, which could overlap with that of the consular service, can be found in Colonial Office classes (lettercode CO) at the Public Record Office, Kew. Records relating to British policy in India are held at the Oriental and India Office Collections of the British Library, 197 Blackfriars Road, London, SE1 8NG. Their holdings include the archives of the East India Company from c. 1600 to 1858, those of the Board of Control, 1784 to 1858, and records of the modern India Office, 1858 to 1947, as well as the Burma Office, 1937 to 1948. These records are also valuable sources for British policy in the middle east and central Asia.

12. Foreign Office General Correspondence

The general correspondence of the Foreign Office contains the most important and extensive documentation of the Foreign Office political departments. These are the papers produced by the Office itself which have accumulated in London. They include originals and copies of despatches from representatives abroad, often with enclosures, reports, translations, newspaper cuttings and private letters sent on for the foreign secretary's information. The files, and before 1906, the volumes containing the correspondence, include the comments of relevant officials and any correspondence that may have been received from other government departments. Copies of the out-going telegrams or letters, along with drafts, can also be found in these records. The general correspondence also includes other material: planning papers which often provided the basis of a formal memorandum presented to the Cabinet by the foreign secretary, draft parliamentary questions for reply in the House of Commons or House of Lords and on which the advice of Foreign Office officials was sought, and records of conversations between senior diplomats or the foreign secretary and foreign envoys resident in London or visiting officials. These last records are the equivalent of the state paper records of the conversations between the secretaries of state and foreign diplomats resident in England and are usually found under the heading 'domestic' in the general correspondence.

The Foreign Office domestic correspondence tends to vary in content but generally contains letters or draft copies of correspondence with other government departments, individuals or outside bodies (usually called 'domestic various'), as well as that with foreign ambassadors or representatives in Britain. There are usually copies of out-going letters and original in-letters. They can be found amongst the correspondence arranged by country before 1906 and the general correspondence in FO 83, FO 95 and FO 96. After 1906 they can be found amongst the general correspondence; see section 12.2. They are also referred to in the various registers compiled in the Foreign Office (see chapter 17). There may also be commercial, treaty and consular domestic correspondence which can be bound separately. Incoming reports from diplomats abroad were generally called 'foreign' while letters from individual persons in the country concerned were called 'foreign various'. These last terms tended to pass out of use as the levels and types of correspondence multiplied during the nineteenth century.

Correspondence relating to a particular issue, conference or long term international question can also be bound up separately. Such papers are labelled as 'cases'. Case volumes can be found amongst the general correspondence at the date at which the issue was decided or when the file was closed. Very long-term questions may have resulted in the creation of separate volumes of records which were bound up annually and placed at the end of the general correspondence for that year, for example papers concerning the Newfoundland fisheries dispute. Some cases are also in FO 83 and FO 97 and there is a manuscript index of cases to 1905 available for consultation in the Reference Room at Kew.

Before 1906 the general correspondence is arranged chronologically in separate classes for each country or area. Because of the various national and geographical changes of the nineteenth century, papers for a particular country or region may be spread through a number of classes. Conversely one class may contain references to many areas. After this date the papers are arranged in general correspondence classes according to content or subject (for example, political, treaty or consular). This means that papers relating to a particular event or country may be found in more than one of the general correspondence classes. The records in each correspondence class may be arranged according to department or administrative sub-division, many of which are geographical. It should be noted that much of the most important correspondence on a particular subject is collected together in confidential print which was produced for circulation in the Foreign Office and to selected outsiders and which may contain copies of documents which have not survived elsewhere (see section 16.4).

12.1 Before 1906

Before 1906 the general correspondence of the political departments of the Foreign Office can be found in individual country classes. These are FO 1 to FO 82, and FO 99 to FO 110. (A full list of the general correspondence classes is available in section 802.9.1 of Part I of the *Current Guide*). Exceptions to this rule are the records of the Chief Clerk's Department in FO 366, covering 1719 to 1959, FO 83, FO 95 and FO 96 (see below), and FO 93 and FO 94 containing treaties and ratifications of treaties (see section 15.1). The general classes also contain the Foreign Office consular, commercial and treaty correspondence for the country concerned. These records are usually bound up as separate volumes and clearly noted in the class lists. Such material is also distinguished in the contemporary indexes and registers. The consular material can also be supplemented using material in FO 83 (see below) and FO 84 (General Correspondence before 1906, Slave Trade, 1816 to 1892).

General and supplementary correspondence can be found in the following classes which provide important early material on the workings of the Foreign Office itself and on specific foreign questions:

FO 83 General Correspondence, Great Britain and General, 1745-1967

This class contains a miscellaneous collection of correspondence, both to home departments and to diplomats abroad, and numerous case papers. The class becomes less useful for the post-1905 period, mainly as a result of registry reforms in that year. It is listed on a subject basis rather than chronologically, and the main divisions are as follows:

a) Miscellaneous correspondence:

Correspondence with government departments, 1745 to 1806; circulars 1777 to 1905, with a separate series of circulars to British ministers and consuls abroad and foreign ministers in London after 1812; domestic various 1773 to 1905, which includes correspondence not classified by a specific country, and annual volumes relating to particular areas or subjects, such as Consular, Commercial, Sanitary, Treaty and Africa.

b) Cases:

Case papers produced by all departments of the Office, except the Chief Clerk's Department, the Slave Trade and African Departments, and arranged under the headings of General, Commercial, Consular, Legal, Library and Treaty appear in this class. The subjects covered, in very broad terms, include arms traffic, aliens, the structure of the diplomatic service, religious and scientific affairs, war and prize law, many aspects of international commercial affairs, (including overseas trade, fishing rights, shipping and industry), consular policy (including the structure of the services and regulations, English churches abroad, marriages abroad, relief and repatriation), law officers' reports, administration of the Foreign Office Library, diplomatic protocol, communications, honours and treaties. Further details of the records contained under these headings are given in the list.

This class also contains royal letters before 1834. Those after 1834 are in FO 95. Some modern drafts of ratifications of treaties, c. 1947 to 1967 are also included.

FO 92 General Correspondence before 1906 Continent Conferences

This class contains correspondence between Viscount Castlereagh and other politicians and diplomats about the course of negotiations prior to the Treaty of Vienna, and papers relating to later conferences, 1814 to 1822. Other papers, dated 1813 to 1822, can be found in FO 139, Continent Conferences (Archives) Correspondence.

FO 139/2 Continent conferences correspondence: report by Viscount Castlereagh on negotiations at Chaumont, 1814

FO 95 Miscellanea, Series I, 1639-1950

This class contains a wide range of material which can be summarised under the following headings:

registers of correspondence 1782 to 1789, 1805 to 1810 and departmental diaries 1806 to 1816 (southern) and 1817 (northern), a further description of which can be found in chapter 17;

supplementary correspondence 1763 to 1857, 1887 to 1918, 1931 to 1938, covering a wide variety of countries and subjects, including the slave trade, treaties, claims, establishments, intercepts and domestic correspondence;

entry books of the secretaries of state, 1789 to 1823, covering domestic and foreign correspondence;

official entry books, 1761 to 1836 (including some domestic entry books, which continue after 1822 in FO 91);

establishment papers, 1772 to 1857 (mainly relating to the foreign service, slave trade and consular matters, see also FO 366, below);

papers of the treaty and royal letter department 1639 to 1942;

library papers, c. 1793 to 1803, mainly memoranda on historical events and treaties;

archives, 1789 to 1840, referring in the main to special missions and commissions;

miscellaneous papers, 1672 to 1720, 1789 to 1829, including the D'Avaux, Bouillon and Calonne papers. (Other Bouillon papers can be found in PC 1, HO 69 and WO 1).

This class is also a good source for intelligence reports on conditions in France during the French Revolutionary and Napoleonic wars. Included are summaries from Paris, the provinces and the ports, which include details of naval and military strengths of the French forces and their movements.

The list for this class is arranged both by piece number and by subject area or by country.

State of the Intelligence up to the 13 June 1790 respecting the Equipments in the Ports of France.

By Lord Robert Fitzgerald's letter dated 4.th June, it appears that the undermentioned Ships had been ordered to be got ready Viz:

	Line	Frigates	Corvettes	Flutes
at Brest	9	9	10	3
Toulon	6	5	3	2
Rochefort	3	5	3	2
L'Orient	3	2	—	—
	21	21	16	7

Captain Dumaresq in his account dated the 1.st of June mentions that the undermentioned Ships were fitting at Brest. Viz:

Le Majesteux	of 110	Guns
Les deux Freres	00	
L'Auguste	00	
L'amerique	74	
Le Trouin	74	
Le Ferme	74	
Le Patriote	74	
Le Superbe	74	
Le Temeraire	74	

and two other Ships of 74 Guns the names of which he does not recollect. — This
account

FO 95/3/1 Supplementary Foreign Office correspondence: survey of French navy and other ships in French ports in 1790

Account does not agree with that trans:
:mitted by Lord Robert, his Lordship includes
Le Citoyen, which Dumaresq does not name,
and neither L'Auguste, Le Superbe or the
two others alluded to by the latter (the names
of which he has forgotten) are inserted in
Lord Robert's List, unless Le Citoyen should
be one of them. from which it may be
concluded that at least three Ships more
have been ordered to be Equipped.

Dumaresq states the Frigates to be

1	La Sibelle	40 Guns
	La Proserpine	40
	Le Didon	40
	La Fidelle	36
5	La Reunion	36
	La Danae	36
	La Pine	36
	La Bellone	36
	La Surveillante	36
10	L'Attalante	36

Corvettes

1	La Ceres	6	Le Cerf
	La Turette		La Pestin
	La Castries		L'Espeigle
	La Ceratte		Le Malouin
5	Le Papillon	10	La Normandie.

FO 95/3/1 Supplementary Foreign Office correspondence: survey of French
navy and other ships in French ports in 1790

FO 96 Miscellanea, Series II, c.1700-1951

This class contains drafts, duplicate despatches, minutes, memoranda, notes of conversations and some documents which can be classed as private correspondence. These documents are arranged by country. Most of the early records relate to South America, the Iberian peninsula and Turkey, with smaller amounts of material concerning the Far East, North America, and Russia, while the later ones refer to Prussia and Austria as well as Turkey. Departmental records include those of the Treaty and Royal Letter Department, the Chief Clerk's Department, and some records of the Slave Trade Department. There are also many important documents illustrating Lord Palmerston's methods as foreign secretary and his relations with the Foreign Office staff.

Other documents include a miscellaneous collection of passports, printed treaties, commercial and slave trade department correspondence and papers, 1819 to 1882, some documents relating to the India Office, 1869 to 1871, addresses to Queen Victoria, draft law reports, dated 1867, miscellaneous petitions, and papers concerning consular protection and property claims. More detailed descriptions of the very varied material in this class can be found in the class list.

FO 97 Supplement to General Correspondence, 1718-1905

This class, arranged by country, comprises similarly varied material, mainly produced by the nineteenth-century political and general departments, and some papers which cannot easily be classified. The records include: treaties, consular correspondence, diplomatic correspondence (relating particularly to African expeditions and annexations), intercepted papers, claims, postal conventions, letter books, a large collection of material on the Schleswig-Holstein question, 1851 to 1864, papers of conferences, *commissions rogatoires*; naval and merchant shipping cases, telegrams, correspondence concerning marriages abroad, Foreign Office establishments and questions of extra-territorial jurisdiction.

There is also some miscellaneous correspondence concerning foreign policy in the nineteenth century in the HD classes which contain information about the expenditure of the secret service vote by the Foreign Office, 1791 to 1909. HD 3, the Permanent Under Secretary's Department Correspondence and Papers, includes material on British diplomacy and surveillance of Russian moves in central Asia, and Anglo-French and Anglo-German relations before 1910. These records also provide information about the use of the secret service fund by the Colonial Office.

Further details about these records can be found in: Louise Atherton, *Top Secret: An Interim Guide to Recent Releases of Intelligence Records at the Public Record Office* (PRO Publications, 1993).

12.2 After 1906

Many of the classes noted above continue after 1906. After c. 1906, the general correspondence is arranged in a series of record classes by function, within which the records may be further divided by department or by geographical area. Some care is needed in using these records as the group of countries in each department varies according to circumstances and internal reforms. To find the departmental organisation of any given year readers should refer to the *Records of the Foreign Office, 1782-1939*, or consult the relevant volume of the *Foreign Office Lists*, which commence in 1852 and were renamed the *Diplomatic Service List* in 1966. The general correspondence classes contain the main series of central Foreign Office records for the twentieth century. Of these, the largest and most important class is FO 371, the political correspondence.

The main general correspondence classes for the twentieth century are as follows:

FO 367 General Correspondence after 1906 Africa, New Series

This class includes the correspondence and papers of the African Department, from 1906 until 1913, when the department was abolished. After 1913 the correspondence of the Africa Departments can be found in FO 371.

FO 366 Chief Clerk's Department Archives

This class contains the papers of the Chief Clerk's Department, created in the nineteenth century, and earlier papers (from 1719). It dealt with the internal administration of the Foreign Office and a variety of other functions. Although the name of the official and the department dealing with the Foreign Office establishment has changed in the modern period, records of the internal structure of the Office continue to be deposited in this class (see section 16.1).

FO 950 General Correspondence, Claims

This class contains records of the Claims Department, created in 1946 to deal with claims made by foreign governments, corporations or individuals for compensation for losses or damages as a result of the Second World War. The records cover 1946 to 1962 so far, and are arranged on a country basis.

FO 368 General Correspondence after 1906 Commercial

Correspondence and papers of the Commercial Department, 1906 to 1920, are held in this class. Earlier commercial material is arranged separately in the country classes of general correspondence before 1906. After 1920 commercial material can be found in a combination of the consular, political and treaty correspondence.

FO 850 General Correspondence after 1906 Communications

Records of the Communications Department from 1936 onwards can be found in this class. Included are files concerning telegrams, the bag service, security, transport between London and missions abroad, and telephone and wireless communication. The department also had duties in safeguarding the security of documents and the Foreign and Diplomatic Service in general. Consequently there are many references in the files to security arrangements in the Foreign Office and embassies and consulates abroad. There are also records concerning cipher systems, suspected bugging devices and arrangements for travel for diplomats and services personnel. Although a Communications Department had been in existence since 1922, records for the period 1927 to 1935 have not survived. Records of the department before 1926 can be found in the Chief Clerk's Department records in FO 366, which also includes early records of messengerial services, which became the responsibility of the Chief clerk from 1854. Other record classes with material relating to communications are FO 83, FO 95, FO 371, FO 351 and FO 900.

FO 369 General Correspondence after 1906, Consular

This class contains correspondence and policy papers of the Consular Department from 1906, which are arranged by date, then by area or country. From 1950 the material is divided up into 'geographical' and 'general' and from 1961 into 'general', 'consular' and 'consular conventions'. The records include references to the protection and welfare of British subjects abroad, the administration and organisation of the service, and reports on local conditions and events. Much of the post-war material concerns the disposal of estates of British subjects abroad, their repatriation, war graves, claims of ill treatment and treatment of prisoners of war. For further details of the matters dealt with by the consular officials see chapter 13.

[Y 2738/15/051]

SECRET

Nature of prefix or Codeword.	Prefix or Codeword.	Position in telegram.
1. Affecting transmission of telegram.	MOST IMMEDIATE IMMEDIATE IMPORTANT DALLY WASTE *JUNGLE**	Preceding address e.g. IMMEDIATE PRODROME LONDON WASTE PRODROME BERNE
2. Denoting telegrams emanating from, or intended for, department other than Foreign Office.	ARFAR ARFAR ENCOM ELPAX MAST FUEL GRUB STOW BRICO PURSA*	First textword (i.e. immediately before No. and date group.)
3. Denoting telegrams to be decyphered by the Head of Mission, diplomatic secretaries, etc.	DEYOU DEDIP	Immediately after No. and date group.
4. Denoting cypher used.	INDIV DIPPX I.D. indicator.	Immediately preceding the first group of recyphered figures. In the case of "INDIV" it should be preceded by the group denoting the table and page used. In the case of the I.D. indicator it should be repeated at the end of the recyphered figures.
5. Denoting telegrams intended for particular officials.	SHACK STOPS }* etc.	Immediately after No. and date group or after codeword "DEYOU" or "DEDIP" when used.

* *Use restricted to certain posts*

FO 850/5   Communications department: guidance paper on use of security prefixes on telegrams by representatives abroad, July 1941

FOREIGN OFFICE, S.W.1. 112

9th November, 1939.

(K 11410/11410/318)

Dear Lady Redesdale,

I had a telephone message from the United States Embassy just after you left for the country this morning saying that your daughter Miss Unity Mitford was in the Surgical Hospital at Munich and was well on the road to recovery. According to the information received by the Embassy, your daughter had attempted to do away with herself on September 3rd.

She had not communicated with the United States Consul-General at Munich, otherwise no doubt we should have had earlier news. As it is I am sure the United States Consular Officials will do all they can in the circumstances, especially as regards getting her sent home when there is an opportunity.

Yours sincerely,

(sd) J.M. Shepherd

Lady Redesdale,
Old Mill Cottage,
High Wycombe.

1939

K

GERMANY.

Registry Number K 11410/11410/318 Position of Miss Unity Mitford in Germany.

FROM Foreign Office
Minutes, Mr.Urquhart.

No.

Dated 5th Sept,1939
Received in Registry 9th Sept,1939

Consular: Germany.

Record of telephone conversation with Lord Redesdale who requested that Vice Consul Weld Forester should telephone him on his arrival home.
Miss Unity Mitford has not left Germany despite all Lord Redesdale's requests.

Last Paper.

References.

(Print.)

(How disposed of.)

(Action completed.) (Index.)

Next Paper.
K/5560

K 11410
9 [...] 1939
10)

FO 369/2563 Consular general correspondence: reports of suicide attempt by Unity Mitford after the outbreak of war with Germany, 9 November 1939

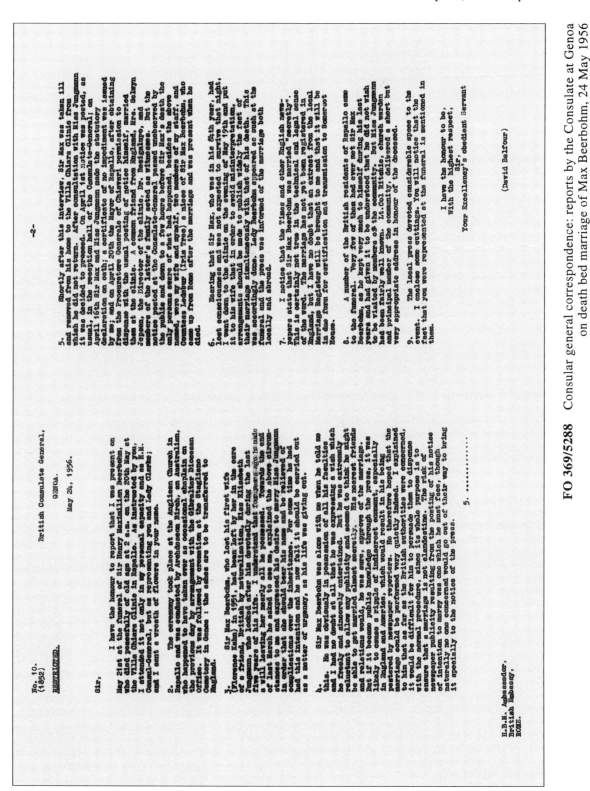

No. 10.
(1852)

RESTRICTED.

British Consulate General,
GENOA.

May 24, 1956.

Sir,

I have the honour to report that I was present on May 21st at the funeral of Sir Henry Maximilian Beerbohm, who died peacefully of old age at 2 a.m. on the 20th May at the Villa Chiara Clinic in Rapallo. As instructed by you, I attended it not only in my personal capacity and as H.M. Consul-General, but as representing you and Lady Clarke; and I sent a wreath of flowers in your name.

2. The ceremony took place at the Anglican Church in Rapallo and was conducted by Archdeacon Hirch, an Australian, who happened to have taken over as occasional chaplain on the previous day by arrangement with the Gibraltar Diocesan office. It was followed by cremation at the Staglieno Cemetery in Genoa: the ashes are to be transferred to England.

3. Sir Max Beerbohm, who lost his first wife (Florence Kahn) in 1951, had been left by her in the care of a friend, British by naturalisation, Miss Elisabeth Jungmann, who looked after him devotedly during the last few years of his life. I understand that towards the end of last March he asked to see me, explained the above circumstances to me and expressed his desire to marry Miss Jungmann in order that she should bear his name and be relieved of complications over the inheritance. For some time he had had this intention and he now felt it should be carried out as a matter of urgency, as his life was giving out.

4. Sir Max Beerbohm was alone with me when he told me this. He was obviously in possession of all his faculties and I had no doubt at all that he was expressing a wish which he freely and sincerely entertained. But he was extremely reluctant to allow any publicity and seemed to think he might be able to get married almost secretly. His nearest friends and relations would, he was sure, approve of the marriage. But if it became public knowledge through the press, it was likely to cause a ripple of indiscreet comment, especially in England and America, which would result in his being pestered by newspaper reporters. He therefore hoped that the marriage could be performed very quietly indeed. I explained to him that as far as the British authorities were concerned, it would be difficult for him to persuade them to dispense with the normal procedure, since its whole purpose is to ensure that a marriage is not clandestine. The risk of newspaper publicity resulting from the posting of his notice of intention to marry was one which he must face, though naturally no one concerned would go out of their way to bring it specially to the notice of the press.

5. ....

-2-

5. Shortly after this interview, Sir Max was taken ill and removed from his home to the Villa Chiara Clinic from which he did not return. After consultation with Miss Jungmann it was decided to proceed. On April 1st notice was posted, as usual, in the reception hall of the Consulate-General; on April 16th Sir Max and Miss Jungmann made the statutory declaration on oath; a certificate of no impediment was issued by me; and on April 20th the Mayor of Rapallo, after obtaining from the Procuratore Generale of Chiavari permission to dispense with the usual posting of notice himself, married them at the clinic. A common friend from England, Mrs. Selwyn Jepson, the Director of the clinic, Dr. Bacigalupo, and members of the latter's family acted as witnesses. But the notice posted at the Consulate-General passed unobserved by the public and down to a few hours before Sir Max's death the only persons aware of what had happened, besides the above named, were my wife and myself, two members of my staff, and Countess Ledebur (Iris Tree) a niece of Sir Max Beerbohm, who came up from Rome after the marriage and was present when he died.

6. Hearing that Sir Max, who was in his 84th year, had lost consciousness and was not expected to survive that night, I went down to the clinic on the evening of May 19th and put it to his wife that in order to avoid misinterpretation their marriage should be made to publish widely the fact of their marriage simultaneously with that of his death. This was accordingly done. Lady Beerbohm appeared as such at the funeral and the press was informed of the marriage both locally and abroad.

7. I notice that the Times and other English newspapers state that Sir Max Beerbohm was married "secretly". This is certainly not true in the technical and legal sense of the word. The marriage has not yet been registered in England, but I have no doubt that in course from the local Marriage Register will be brought to me and that it will be in due form for certification and transmission to Somerset House.

8. A number of the British residents of Rapallo came to the funeral. Very few of them had ever met Sir Max Beerbohm, as he kept very much to himself during his last years and had given it to be understood that he did not wish to be visited by members of the community. But Miss Jungmann had been fairly well known. Lt.Col Ritchie, church warden and principal member of the community, delivered a short but very appropriate address in honour of the deceased.

9. The local press devoted considerable space to the event. I enclose some cuttings. You will notice that the fact that you were represented at the funeral is mentioned in them.

I have the honour to be,
With the highest respect,
Sir,
Your Excellency's obedient Servant

(David Belfour)

H.B.M. Ambassador,
British Embassy,
ROME.

FO 369/5288 Consular general correspondence: reports by the Consulate at Genoa on death bed marriage of Max Beerbohm, 24 May 1956

FO 382 General Correspondence after 1906, Contraband

This class contains records of the Contraband Department of the Foreign Office and the Ministry of Blockade, 1915 to 1920. The records are arranged by date, country or region, as well as by subject, for example, mails, tonnage and censorship.

FO 924 General Correspondence after 1906, Cultural Relations

Included in this class are the correspondence and policy papers of the Cultural Relations Department, which was established in 1944. Much of its work concerns liaison with the British Council, which was established in 1934, and other international cultural and educational organisations. File subjects include British Council administration and organisation, exhibitions, cultural conventions, educational conferences, cultural institutes and lecture tours. There are also references to the pre-war Travel and Industrial Association, British participation in United Nations cultural organisations and to student exchanges. During the Second World War liaison with the British Council was the responsibility of the Library (see FO 370, described below).

FO 627 General Correspondence after 1906, Dominions Information

This class contains records of the Dominions Information Department which was established in 1926 shortly after the Dominions Office, and which carried out political liaison functions. Its records cover 1929 to 1933. See also FO 372.

FO 953 Foreign Publicity from 1947

This class contains material produced by the series of Information Departments created in the Foreign Office which were responsible for publicity and cultural propaganda about Britain abroad from 1947. The records deal with general policy matters and with activities in individual countries conducted by the country sections. Included are quarterly and monthly country reports, and administrative and policy files. This class also contains information on the role of BBC broadcasting abroad, and guidance for diplomatic and consular staff on publicity for specific events or issues, such as counter measures against Soviet propaganda in the 1950s or the introduction of Marshall aid into Europe. Earlier material relating to foreign publicity and propaganda work can be found amongst the records of the Ministry of Information (INF classes), in FO 930 from 1938 to 1947 and in records of the News Department, as described below. Other material can be found in FO 972, foreign policy documents, FO 973, background briefs, FO 975, information reports, and in the records of the British Council (BW lettercode classes). FO 972 and FO 973 are not 30 year closure classes so the information they contain is relatively up to date.

CONFIDENTIAL

> RECEIVED IN
> ARCHIVES
> 23 JUN 1961
>
> CR 13832/2.

The Dancer Nereyev

Mr Hochhauser has just consulted me about the dancer Nereyev who defected from the Kirov Ballet Company at Paris Airport on the way to London last week. The press announces that Nereyev has now signed up with the Marquis de Cuevas Company for a very large sum and is to appear in Paris in "The Sleeping Beauty" on the very night when he should have made his <u>début</u> in that ballet at Covent Garden.

2. Mr Hochhauser tells me in strict confidence that both the Kirov Ballet and the Soviet Chargé d'Affaires are shocked at the way the Soviet security people handled Nereyev and still have hopes of getting him back. Apparently Nereyev had no intention of seeking political asylum and no interest in political matters: his whole life is bound up with the ballet and his greatest ambition was to appear at Covent Garden. In Paris he became rather too friendly with people whom the Party frowned upon (presumably émigrés) and the watch-dogs attached to the Company decided to send him home. Nothing was said to him until the Company reached the airport to fly to London. When the watch-dogs then tried to take him away he very naturally reacted as reported in the press.

3. The Kirov Company are under contract to Mr Hochhauser to produce certain specified dancers including Nereyev at Covent Garden, so that he can take proceedings against them for breach of contract. He does not wish to do this since it would help no one and only cause ill-feeling. He does, however, wish to stop Nereyev appearing in the same rôle with a rival company and intends to instruct his lawyers to apply for an injunction. He asked me whether I thought he would be criticised here for so doing.

4. I said that I could not give an official Foreign Office view but that in my personal opinion he would be fully justified in taking legal steps to prevent Nereyev breaking his contract, provided he did nothing that could be interpreted as an attempt to force him to rejoin the Kirov Company. The one thing we should want to avoid was having Nereyev come here and then try to defect again.

5. If Mr Hochhauser succeeds with his injunction Nereyev will no doubt be under strong pressure from the Kirov Company to rejoin them: he has already been assured that he would still be welcome, and that, for what it is worth, he will not be penalised. From our point of view it would be better if he stayed in Paris and saved us the risk of a possible second defection. But I do not see that we can advise Mr Hochhauser not to take the obvious legal steps to protect his interests <u>vis-à-vis</u> his French rivals.

(R.L. Speaight)

June 20, 1961

Mr F.R.H. Murray
 Copied to: Mr R.H. Mason
News Department, Security Dept.
 I R D   CONFIDENTIAL

I agree but we ... cannot

FO 924/1399 Cultural relations from 1944: report on the defection of Rudolf Nureyev and resulting contract liabilities of the Kirov Ballet, 20 June 1961.

En Clair   DEPARTMENTAL DISTRIBUTION

FROM FOREIGN OFFICE TO PARIS

No. 259
2nd March, 1950.   D. 3.45 p.m. 2nd March, 1950.

AND ALSO TO:-
   Rome No. 366, Wahnerheide, The Hague No.117,
   Brussels No. 90, Stockholm No.79, Oslo No.75,
   Copenhagen No. 76, Singapore No. 275, Cairo No.367.

MANDATE

   Following points may be useful if you are called upon to comment on Fuchs trial.

2. Attorney General (prosecuting) and defense counsel both drew attention to the tragedy of this brilliant scientist who had been led by allegiance to the Communist Party to give information to Communist agents in breach of his oath of secrecy and the oath of allegiance taken at the time of his naturalisation in 1942. Under the influence of the "deep-rooted firmness" and decency of the people with whom he worked in England, he had gradually come to doubt the rightness of this allegiance and to disapprove of many actions of the Soviet Government and Communist Party, and had returned to the conviction that a man must be free to question and reject party decisions. He had reduced and then discontinued the supply of information, and eventually made a full and voluntary confession. Thereafter he gave every possible help to the authorities to minimise the effects of his treachery.

3. It was made clear at the trial that until Fuchs made his statement there was no evidence on which he could have been arrested, although there had been indications that serious leaks had occurred when the British Research Mission, of which Fuchs was a member, was in the United States. Fuchs was not a member of the British Communist Party and since his arrival in this country in 1933 had taken no apparent interest in politics.

/4. Attorney General

Foreign Office telegram No. 259 to Paris

(2)

4. Attorney General emphasised, by way of contrast with trials in satellite countries, that Fuchs' statement was made when he was still free to come and go, so that there could be no question of its having been extorted from him. He was brought before a magistrates' court the day after arrest and to trial within a month.

DISTRIBUTED TO:-

Information Research Department
Economic Relations Department
Mr. E.R.M. Warner
Information Policy Department
Cultural Relations Department
News Department
Director General C.O.I.

XXXXX

FO 953/642 Foreign publicity: guidance telegram for representatives abroad in the event of being called upon to comment on the Fuchs trial, 2 March 1950

FO 370 General Correspondence, Library from 1906

Included in this class are papers and correspondence of the Foreign Office Library, which from 1906 was responsible for the Registry. Historically its functions have been varied, for example it had charge of the messenger service from 1824 to 1854. In 1946 the Registry became known formally as the Archives Department. The Library received requests for information or publications from other departments and from abroad, as well as advice on archival and publishing matters. As a result the records contain information on a huge variety of topics. Other records relating to the Library and its work can be found in FO 83, FO 95, FO 351, and FO 366. The Library series of registers and indexes to general correspondence are in FO 802 with microfilm copies in FO 605; see chapter 17.

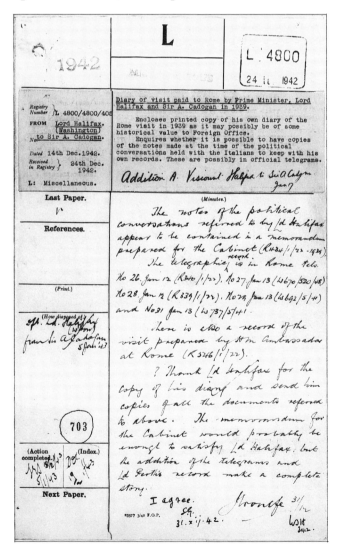

FO 370/703   General correspondence Library: enclosure of copy of diary by Lord Halifax, the Ambassador to the USA, dated January 1939, of his visit to Italy, and a request for access to records, 14 December 1942

FO 395 General Correspondence after 1906, News

This class includes correspondence and policy papers of the News Department which was formed in 1914. Its functions were to monitor domestic and foreign newspapers, collect information from the foreign press and to assist in the release of official information to the national press. It also had a role in the provision of publicity for Britain overseas. The records consist of files of reports, policy papers and correspondence, and can include press cuttings, notes of cultural exchanges, lecture tours and film production and correspondence with British Council officials. The records in this class cover the period 1916 to 1939. Material for the period 1914 to 1915 can be found in FO 371, as can that for the Second World War when some departmental functions were lost to the Ministry of Information. Some press summaries of foreign material can be found in FO 899, Cabinet papers, 1915 to 1917. Material after 1939 can be found in FO 953 and FO 930 (see above).

FO 371 General Correspondence, Political from 1906

This class contains the correspondence, policy papers, memoranda and minutes of the political departments of the Foreign Office. It is the most important class for the diplomatic historian and contains examples of all the documents described in detail at the start of this section (see section 12). The files in FO 371 are those of the political and subject departments of the Foreign Office itself, and as such, contain the main policy papers of the senior planning officials in London. They often include notes of the opinions of Cabinet ministers, Cabinet papers, intelligence reports and correspondence, as well as providing evidence on the interaction between the foreign secretary and his diplomatic advisers. These files are the main source to show how the Foreign Office officials in their departments reached a policy position and what action, if any, resulted from it. Also included in this class are the records of the War Department, 1914 to 1920, and the Political Intelligence Department, 1918 to 1920.

M. Pineau and I received the EGYPTIAN AMBASSADOR and transmitted to him the Note destined for the Egyptian Government.

2. On reading it the Ambassador said he was horrified at its contents. He did not consider this was a note which should be addressed to a country which was the victim of aggression. As an Egyptian he felt that the demands were quite unacceptable. I asked him which demands were unacceptable. He replied the third. He went on to say that it was unworthy of the authors of the Tripartite Declaration to address this ultimatum to Egypt and he wondered whether he ought even to receive the Note. M. Pineau said that Egypt had really repudiated the Tripartite Declaration and had no business to invoke it. He strongly advised the Egyptian Ambassador to transmit the communication and give his government an opportunity of deliberation. The Ambassador said he would do so.

3. I then told the Ambassador that it was our intention to exercise our right under the 1888 Treaty to send a warship to Port Said. He said he took note of that.

4. The Ambassador after making a further protest against the contents of the Note, took his leave.

I. Kirkpatrick
October 30, 1956.

Distribution:

African Department (to enter)

Copies to:

    Private Secretary
    Lord Reading
    Mr. Nutting
    Mr. Dodds-Parker
    Lord John Hope
    Mr. Dean
    Mr. Reilly
    Sir J. Ward
    Mr. Gore-Booth
    Mr. A. D. M. Ross

    Levent Department.

J **JE1094/3**

AFRICAN DEPARTMENT

FROM
F.O. Minute
Sir J. Kirkpatrick

No.

Dated Oct. 30

Received in Registry—

Anglo-French ultimatum to Egypt.

Report interview which M. Pineau had with the Egyptian Ambassador, who was given the Note destined for the Egyptian Govt.

References to former relevant papers

MINUTES

(Print)

(How disposed of)

(Action completed)

References to later relevant papers

49957

FO 371/118902 General political correspondence: file cover with enclosed minute by Sir Ivone Kirkpatrick on conversation of himself and M. Pineau, with the Egyptian ambassador prior to the Angol-French landings and the Suez crisis, 30 October 1956

FO 383 General Correspondence after 1906, Prisoners

This class includes records of the Prisoners of War and Aliens Department, established in 1915 to deal with all questions relating to conditions of prisoners, repatriation and general policy. The records are arranged by date and by country, with a general and miscellaneous section and they cover 1915 to 1919.

FO 372 General Correspondence after 1906, Treaty

Included in this class are the papers of the Treaty Department of the Foreign Office, from 1906 onwards. The department is not concerned with the actual negotiating of treaties, but with the process of putting them into effect. The Treaty Department has dealt with a wide range of duties during the course of its history. Consequently the records include references to most of them, for example, the preparation of diplomatic documents and treaties, protocol and precedence, orders and medals, honorary awards and diplomatic privilege. The first Treaty Department was thought to have been formed from c. 1813 and has occasionally formed part of the Chief Clerk's Department. By 1891 the department also dealt with commissions, exequaturs, copyright, naturalisations, extraditions and passports, and, from 1894, postal treaties and conferences. The records concerning naturalisations and extraditions refer mainly to matters of policy rather than to individuals, but there are exceptions. This class also contains information on a variety of other subjects including royal marriages, marriage law abroad, nationality questions and diplomatic and consular appointments. References to Dominions intelligence reports can also be found amongst these records.

Early material of the Treaty Department can be found in the individual country classes before 1906, where it is listed under the heading 'treaty' and bound separately. Other records can be found in FO 366, the records of the Chief Clerk, whose department had responsibility for treaties to 1854. FO 95 also contains treaty department memoranda, 1860 to c. 1925, and treaty papers, c. 1793 to 1797, 1801 to 1803, and 1805 to 1837. FO 372 also includes records of the Prize Court Department, 1914 to 1920, and the Dominions Information Department, 1926 to 1928.

180

MEMORANDUM.

THE Under-Secretary of State for Foreign Affairs presents his compliments to the King's Private Secretary, and is directed by the Secretary of State to inform him that His Majesty has been pleased to grant restricted permission to the under-mentioned person to accept and wear the decoration indicated against his name , conferred upon him by His Majesty the King of Italy in recognition of his services to the Italian film industry.

Alexander Korda, Esq.,   Commander of the Order
Managing Director of London   of the Crown of Italy.
Film Productions, Ltd.

It is accordingly requested that the customary formal letter acquainting Mr. Korda of the grant of such restricted permission may be prepared and forwarded to this Office for transmission to him , and that this Memorandum may be marked below as having been acted on and returned to the Treaty Department, Foreign Office, for record.

Foreign Office,
11th January , 193 8.

Date of Letter sent........13th January, 1938..........

Initial of Private Secretary..............*A.k.*................

3943 15309

FO 372/3261   Treaty Department file: authorisation for Alexander Korda to wear a decoration awarded by the King of Italy, 11 January 1938

13. Embassy and Consular Archives

Embassy and Consular archives are made up of the papers produced by the staff of the permanent embassies and consulates situated abroad. They consist of:

despatches and telegrams received by the missions from the Foreign Office in London and draft despatches for reply;

correspondence with the foreign ministry of the country to which they were accredited;

correspondence with individuals and organisations, including British officials and representatives of business interests in the country; (this correspondence between the embassy and the consular posts for the country concerned is not duplicated elsewhere);

letterbooks of outgoing correspondence compiled at the embassy and consulate, but which fell into disuse as a form of record by the late nineteenth and early twentieth centuries;

registers of incoming and outgoing correspondence;

miscellaneous material, including registers of births, marriages and deaths, shipping regulation papers, legal records and others.

To some extent embassy and consular material can be supplemented using the general correspondence of the Foreign Office by using the 'central' and 'local' archives in conjunction. The two sets of records complement rather than duplicate each other in their contents. Often the embassy and consular material will provide a very different interpretation of events from the Foreign Office perspective and it is always useful to consult when researching a particular episode. It should also be noted that until c. 1815 French was still the most commonly used language in consular affairs as well as diplomatic.

As a result of various nineteenth-century acts of Parliament, chiefly the registration acts of 1849 and the Consular Marriage Act of that year, the consuls had statutory duties in the return of records of births, marriages and deaths of Britons abroad. Returns were made to the Registrar General in London, and it became usual for the embassies and consulates to keep registers. Many of these have survived and can now be found in the country series of embassy and consular archives, and in the records of the Registrar General now deposited in the PRO which can be consulted at Chancery Lane. General correspondence on these duties and returns of marriages overseas can be found in FO 83, for the period 1814 to 1905, and supplementary material is in FO 97, for 1873 to 1880. These latter records often have case papers on particular marriages where a legal point was involved, for example mixed marriages or cases of desertion abroad. Indexes by name to consular registers of births, marriages and deaths, 1849 to 1965, are available at the General Register Office, St. Catherine's House, 10 Kingsway, London WC2B 6JP. These overlap with PRO holdings.

For further guidance about these records, you should consult Chapter 4 of *Tracing Your Ancestors in the Public Record Office*, 4th edition, by Amanda Bevan and Andrea Duncan (London, HMSO 1990), which includes a list of Foreign Office classes containing such registers. Information about these records and those held elsewhere can also be found in G Yeo, *The British Overseas* (Guildhall Library Guide 2, 2nd edition, London, 1988, revised edition forthcoming). There is also an index to registers of births, marriages and deaths overseas in the 'FO Index' which is a separate volume at the start of the series of Foreign Office lists which is available in the Reference Rooms at Kew and at Chancery Lane. The index provides a list of countries and references. It does not contain an index of names which may occur in these records.

The embassy and consular records also contain a large amount of miscellaneous material, for example consular court records where such a court was held under extra-territorial privilege, commercial and business papers and various records concerning British subjects abroad, such as wills, estate papers and deeds, and papers relating to British churches and cemeteries. Some consular court records contain entry books of civil and criminal cases, correspondence and registration documents of limited companies and inquests. Some consuls also kept official diaries, in which they recorded events of note including births and deaths in leading families, and trading and shipping conditions where the consulate was based at a port. Some of these have survived amongst the consular archives.

As the consuls had various duties concerning the collection of port dues, and in shipping and merchant seamen regulation, there are also miscellaneous papers touching on maritime administration. The records of a particular consulate may include ships agreements, articles and lists (for example, FO 267, the Archangel consular records class). There may be local political summaries and trade reports. Archives of missions and consulates can also include confidential print (usually sets of annual reports on various countries for a given year), assorted types of entry books, accounts, passport registers and some case volumes. While not perhaps a consular archive as such, the Foreign Office records also contain records of the English church at the Hague, 1658 to 1882, which are composed of inventories, minutes of the consistory courts and various legal papers which are a useful source of information about the community abroad (FO 259).

A note of caution should be sounded, however. There are substantial gaps in the embassy and consular archives due to destruction through diplomatic crisis, war or natural disaster, and for some posts no material survives at all. The embassy and consular records also were vulnerable to fires, mould, pests and a casual attitude towards record keeping. There are significant gaps for the Second World War period due to destruction; for example much of the material from the British embassy in Poland for 1931 to 1939 was destroyed during the invasion by German forces in September 1939. In some cases registers have survived where the correspondence has been destroyed, for example in the Embassy and Consular archives Belgium, 1925 to 1938. Some consular material captured by the German armies has survived however; FO 952, Embassy and Consular Archives Norway includes records of the consulates at Bergen, Haugesund, Tromso and Stavanger which were captured in April 1940.

The embassy and consular records are unweeded and bound in volumes from the nineteenth to the early twentieth centuries. The post-war consular material is mainly arranged by subject and has been subjected to weeding, with the result that the consular material is of decreasing utility to the researcher as regards the very modern period.

Most missions and consulates kept entry books of correspondence from the 1820s. With the reform of the registration systems in the Foreign Office from c. 1860, it also became more common for registers to be kept. Many missions kept entry books until the late nineteenth century or early twentieth century, when the keeping of such records fell into disuse, mainly because of the growing numbers and speed of communications. Not all of these registers have survived for the same reasons as given above, butwhere they do they are a useful source for outgoing correspondence.

In the eighteenth and nineteenth centuries consular officials could also correspond directly with the Board of Trade which had a general oversight of trading and commercial affairs. The Foreign Office continued to send consular despatches on to the Board for much of the nineteenth century. Further details of consular work and commercial relations can therefore be found among the records of the Board of Trade, in particular in BT 1, BT 2, BT 6, BT 10 and BT 11. In the twentieth century the Board of Trade and its successors have continued to be involved in international commercial affairs, particularly economic treaties and international economic organisations. Relevant classes include BT 205, BT 269 and BT 274. The Treasury records also contain a wealth of information on international trading and finance. Examples of consular seals used in the transaction of official business have also been preserved; FO 365 includes examples of such seals from the late eighteenth century to c. 1947, as well as seals of foreign secretaries and commissions, 1783 to 1865.

Embassy and consular archives for particular countries can be identified using Section 802.9.3 of Part 1 of the *Current Guide*, 'Embassy and Consular Archives'. They can also be traced using the 'FO Index'. The records are arranged according to the country exercising sovereignty at the time and are grouped with the records of the embassy for that state. Because of the changing nature of diplomatic and consular representation and changes in internal sovereignties, readers should take account of the fact that there may be overlapping between embassy and consular material in separate classes: for example, the various states in the Balkans which were formerly part of the Ottoman Empire.

April 30, 1856.

Shalom Benmooyal, a British subject, and Rachel Mooyal a Moorish subject, presented themselves at the office of the British Vice Consul at Rabat, and stated that they had been married on the 25th March 1856, ~~and~~ they produced a document drawn up and signed by two Jewish Rabbi's dated the 18th Hodis Adar Seeny (25th March) certifying that they the said Shalom Benmooyal and Rachel Mooyal had been married on that date. —

August 2.

Arrived off Rabat the Russian Government Steamer "Danzig" at about half past five A.m., at about half past ten two boats from the "Danzig" with fourteen officers came to the landing place, one of the officers calling himself Commander Barnim, presented a Bill of Health given at Plymouth, by which it appeared that the "Danzig" was commanded by Prince William Von Hessen. Commander Barnim mentioned, that he then commanded the "Danzig", the Prince having

FO 442/8   Embassy and consular archives, Morocco: official diary of the consul, Rabat, giving details about the British community and foreign shipping, entries for April and August 1856

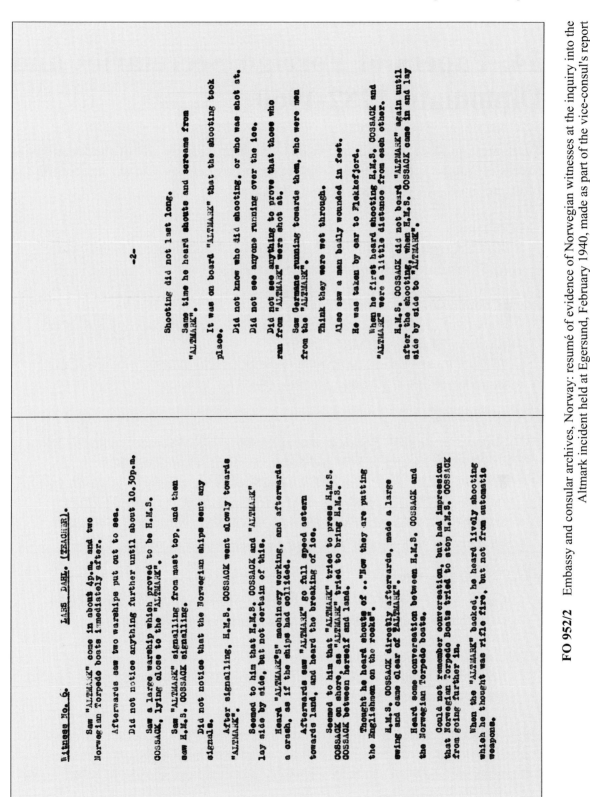

Witness No. 5.   LARS DAHL. (TEACHER).

Saw "ALTMARK" come in about 4p.m. and two Norwegian Torpedo boats immediately after.

Afterwards saw two warships put out to sea.

Did not notice anything further until about 10.30p.m.

Saw a large warship which proved to be H.M.S. COSSACK, lying close to the "ALTMARK".

Saw "ALTMARK" signalling from mast top, and then saw H.M.S. COSSACK signalling.

Did not notice that the Norwegian ships sent any signals.

After signalling, H.M.S. COSSACK went slowly towards "ALTMARK".

Seemed to him that H.M.S. COSSACK and "ALTMARK" lay side by side, but not certain of this.

Heard "ALTMARK'S" machinery working, and afterwards a crash, as if the ships had collided.

Afterwards saw "ALTMARK" go full speed astern towards land, and heard the breaking of ice.

Seemed to him that "ALTMARK" tried to press H.M.S. COSSACK on shore, as "ALTMARK" tried to bring H.M.S. COSSACK between herself and land.

Thought he heard shouts of .. "Now they are putting the Englishmen on the rocks".

H.M.S. COSSACK directly afterwards, made a large swing and came clear of "ALTMARK".

Heard some conversation between H.M.S. COSSACK and the Norwegian Torpedo boats.

Could not remember conversation, but had impression that Norwegian Torpedo Boats tried to stop H.M.S. COSSACK from going further in.

When the "ALTMARK" backed, he heard lively shooting which he thought was rifle fire, but not from automatic weapons.

-2-

Shooting did not last long.

Same time he heard shouts and screams from "ALTMARK".

It was on board "ALTMARK" that the shooting took place.

Did not know who did shooting, or who was shot at.

Did not see anyone running over the ice.

Did not see anything to prove that those who ran from "ALTMARK" were shot at.

Saw Germans running towards them, who were men from the "ALTMARK".

Think they were wet through.

Also saw a man badly wounded in feet.

He was taken by car to Flekkefjord.

When he first heard shooting H.M.S. COSSACK and "ALTMARK" were a little distance from each other.

H.M.S. COSSACK did not board "ALTMARK" again until after the shooting, when H.M.S. COSSACK came in and lay side by side to "ALTMARK".

FO 952/2 Embassy and consular archives, Norway: resumé of evidence of Norwegian witnesses at the inquiry into the Altmark incident held at Egersund, February 1940, made as part of the vice-consul's report

14. Papers of Foreign Secretaries and Diplomats: 1782-1960

There are a number of published works which provide details of the locations of papers of foreign secretaries and diplomats in this country and abroad both in the PRO and in other repositories. Useful titles are:

J M Collinge

> *Foreign Office Officials 1782-1870, Office Holders in Modern Britain VIII* (Institute of Historical Research, 1979)

Royal Commission on Historical Manuscripts

> *Papers of British Politicians 1782-1900, Guides to Sources for British History 7* (London, HMSO, 1989)
> *Private Papers of British Diplomats, 1782-1900, Guides to Sources for British History 4* (London, HMSO, 1985)

C Cook

> *Sources in English Political History 1900-1951*, volume 2, *A Guide to the Private Papers of Selected Public Servants* (London, 1975)
> *Sources in English Political History 1900-1951*, volume 3, *A Guide to the Private Papers of Members of Parliament A-K* (London, 1977)
> *Sources in English Political History 1900-1951*, volume 4, *A Guide to the Private Papers of Members of Parliament L-Z* (London, 1977)

C Hazlehurst and C Wood

> *Guide to the Papers of British Cabinet Ministers, 1900-1951* (Royal Historical Society, London 1974, new edition forthcoming).

S T Bindoff, E F Malcolm, C K Webster, eds.

> *British Diplomatic Representatives 1789-1852*, Camden Society, 3rd Series (London, 1934)

Many official papers of diplomats survive in the PRO, whether in classes of deposited private collections or classes of private office papers. Some private collections include what can be described as private letters relating to public affairs.

They may contain copies of official telegrams or memoranda. Many private diplomatic papers are still in private hands or have been deposited in local and national repositories; for locations readers should consult the National Register of Archives as above (Chapter 8). Official papers of secretaries of state, diplomats and officials which were surrendered to the Foreign Office on retirement or on leaving the service are to be found mainly in FO 800, with deposited collections in PRO 30 classes. To trace the papers of diplomats by name the index to the *Current Guide* can also be used.

The main collections of private papers of British foreign secretaries, under-secretaries, diplomats and consular officials (excluding their papers in general correspondence classes) are as follows. Where dates are given they refer to the span of material available in the PRO. For biographical detail refer to the *Records of the Foreign Office, 1782-1939*, the introductory notes to the class lists, the *Dictionary of National Biography* and the Foreign Office *Diplomatic Lists* for career posting of diplomatic and consular staff.

FO 363	Abbott, Charles, 3rd baron Tenterden, 1873-1882
FO 95/503-4	Adair, Sir Robert, 1831-1837,
FO 261/1-7 PRO 30/26/72	Ainslie, Sir Robert 1776-1794, 1783-1787
FO 800/244-248	Alston, Sir Beilby Francis, 1908-1915
	Amberley, viscount, *see* Russell, Lord John
	Ampthill, 1st Lord, *see* Russell, Odo
PRO 30/40	Ardagh, Major General Sir John, 1862-1906, 1909
FO 355	Aston, Sir Arthur, 1827-1843
	Avon, 1st earl of, *see* Eden, Sir (Robert) Anthony
FO 323/6	Backhouse, John, 1834
FO 800/199-217, PRO 30/60	Balfour, Sir Arthur James, 1st earl, c.1887-1891, 1916-1922

PRO 30/60	Balfour, Gerald William, 2nd earl Balfour, [1880]-1907
FO 800/433	Balfour, Sir John, 1940-1941
FO 633	Baring, Evelyn, 1st earl of Cromer, 1840-1929
FO 800/852	Baxter, Charles William, 1920-1921
FO 800/159-191	Bertie, Sir Francis, Lord Bertie of Thame, 1896-1919
FO 800/434-522	Bevin, Ernest, 1945-1951
FO 356	Bloomfield, General Benjamin, 1823-1871
PRO 30/67	Brodrick, William, 1st Earl Middleton 1885-1941
FO 800/331-335	Bryce, Sir James, viscount Dechmont, 1904-1921
FO 800/232	Bulwer, Sir Henry, 1848-1851
FO 800/419-29, 523-528, 533-613	Butler, Sir Nevile, 1916, [1927]-1937, 1940-1941, 1944-1954
FO 800/293-294	Cadogan, Sir Alexander, 1934-1936, 1936-1939
FO 800/229-231	Canning, George, 1824-1827
FO 352	Canning, Stratford (Lord Stratford de Redcliffe), 1778-1873
FO 323/3	Caradoc, Lt. Col. Hon. J H, 1834-1835
	Carnarvon, 4th earl, *see* Molyneux, Henry Howard
	Cave papers, see Douglas Arthur Snape
	Cecil, 1st viscount, see Gascoyne-Cecil, Lord Robert
FO 800/256-263	Chamberlain, Sir Austen, 1924-1929
	Chelwood, 1st viscount, *see* Gascoyne-Cecil, Robert

Clarendon, 4th earl, *see* Villiers, George

FO 800/298-303 Clark-Kerr, Archibald, Lord Inverchapel, 1935-1939, 1942-1949

FO 794/8 Clerk, Sir George Russell, 1921, 1934

FO 660/107-199 Cooper, Sir Alfred Duff, 1st viscount Norwich, 1944-1945

PRO 30/26/124 Corbett, Sir Vincent, 1892-1893

PRO 30/11 Cornwallis, Charles, family papers 1614-1854

Cowley papers, see Henry Wellesley, 1st Baron,
Henry Richard Wellesley, 2nd baron and 1st earl, and Col.
Hon Frederick Wellesley

Cranbourne, viscount, *see* Gascoyne-Cecil, Robert

FO 800/330 Crewe-Milnes, Robert, 1st Marquess of Crewe, 1926

CAB 127/57-154 Cripps, Sir Stafford, 1932-1950

Cromer, 1st earl of, *see* Baring, Evelyn

FO 800/243
FO 794/2 Crowe, Sir Eyre, 1907-1925

FO 800/114 Currie, Sir Phillip, 1893-1896

FO 800/28, 147-158 Curzon, George Nathaniel, 5th baron Scarsdale, Marquess
Curzon of Kedleston, 1886-1897, 1895-1898, 1919-1924

Cushenden, 1st Baron, *see* McNeil, Ronald

PRO 30/58 Dacres Adams, William, 1676, 1783-1856

Dechmont, viscount, *see* Bryce, Sir James

FO 794/3 Dering, Sir Herbert, 1915-1918

FO 800/197   Dormer, Cecil, c. 1915-1919

PRO 30/7   Douglas, Arthur Snape, 1811-1914, 1816-1818, 1822

FO 800/329,   Drummond, Sir Eric, c. 1915-1921
383-385

FO 594   Eden, Sir (Robert) Anthony, 1st earl of Avon,
FO 800/750-851   1935-1946, 1951-1955

FO 800/255   Elliot, Sir Charles, 1904-1919, 1924-1925
FO 794/1

FO 360   Ellis, Charles, Augustus, Lord Howard de Walden, 1817-1834

FO 800/235-239   Errington, George, 1881-1885

FO 800/25-28   Fergusson, Sir James, 1886-1897

FO 800/115-146   Fitzmaurice, Henry Charles Keith Petty, 5th marquess of
     Lansdowne, 1898-1913

FO 348   Foresti, Spiridion, 1793-1813

FO 97/16-19   Fox, Henry Stephen, 1836-1844

FO 800/296   Gascoyne-Cecil, Robert, viscount Cranbourne, 5th marquess
     of Salisbury, 1935-1938

FO 800/195-198   Gascoyne-Cecil, Lord Robert, 1st Viscount Cecil of
     Chelwood, 1915-1919

FO 794/6A   Graham, Sir Ronald, 1918, 1929-1933

     Granville papers, see Leveson-Gower (Granville Leveson-
     Gower and Granville George Leveson-Gower).

FO 800/35-113   Grey, Sir Edward, 1892-1895, 1905-1916

     Halifax, third viscount, *see* Wood, Edward

65

Rab very kindly sent me a word by Harold Caccia, and I will do my best to carry through this plan if it is thought useful. Maybe you could have a word with Rab and Harry about it. But I am afraid that in any event much must depend upon the situation here at the time.

The French news seems so much worse. And goodness knows where we may be by Friday!

Yours ever

(Sgd) ANTHONY EDEN

United Kingdom Delegation to the
Geneva Conference.   64

28.

May D, 1954.   FE/54/41

STRICTLY PERSONAL

I have thought much about you all at home, and I am afraid that you in particular must have had a strenuous time trying to keep our majority in being with so many absentees, including myself.

This is the most difficult conference I have ever known, but I hope that this week we may really be able to get things moving. I do not believe that there is any real hope of an agreement on Korea, but at least, we shall be able to table some reputable proposals, and then the Communists can take them or leave them.

Indo-China is much more difficult. Bidault has his difficulties at home, and hitherto the American attitude has been unrealistic. Because the French clearly will not go on fighting indefinitely, the Americans have not been willing to face any possible compromise.

It is however just possible that I might be able to get away on Friday for a long weekend, returning here on Monday afternoon or Tuesday morning. If so, I should hope it might be possible to get some clarification of plan, probably by means of a renewal of the meeting of five or six. We did decide to adjourn it until May.

our domestic

/Rab

The Rght. Honourable
R.G.A. Buchan-Rayburn, M.P.

FO 800/785 Private papers: Anthony Eden and Far Eastern affairs, 1954: comments on the Geneva Conference shortly after the fall of Dien Bien Phu, French Indo-China

FO 391	Hammond, Lord Edmund, 1st baron, 1831-1834, 1854-1885
FO 95/502,508-509	Hammond, George, 1789-1791, 1796-1797
FO 800/24, 192,197	Hardinge, Sir Charles, 1906-1911, 1915-1919
FO 800/250	Harmsworth, Cecil, 1919
FO 800/194	Harvey, Sir Henry, c. 1913-1914
FO 800/662	Helm, Sir Knox, 1954-1956
FO 800/280-284	Henderson, Arthur, 1929-1931
FO 357	Henderson, James, 1818-1831
FO 800/264-271, FO 794/10	Henderson, Sir Nevile, 1923, 1924-1941
FO 351	Hertslet, Lewis, 1730-1854
FO 528	Hervey, Lord John Augustus, 1778-1794
FO 528	Hervey, Lord William, 1830-1840
FO 800/295	Hoare, Sir Samuel, 1935
	Howard de Walden, Lord, see Ellis, Charles Augustus
	Hyde, 4th baron, *see* Villiers, George
	Inverchapel, Lord, *see* Clerk-Kerr, Sir Archibald
FO 800/222-226	Isaacs, Sir Rufus, Lord Reading, 1918-1919, 1931
FO 353	Jackson papers, (Francis James Jackson, 1770-1841 and Sir George Jackson, 1785-1861)
PRO 30/26/70/1-3	Johnson, John Mordaunt, 1809-1814
FO 350	Jordan, Sir John, 1901-1919

PRO 30/26/85	Macleod, Sir James MacIver, 1895-1929
FO 800/663-690 FO 660	Macmillan, Harold, 1943-1945, 1955
FO 800/432, 614-626	Makins, Sir Roger, 1st baron Sherfield, 1936-1953,
FO 343	Malet, Sir Edward, 1884-1895
	Malmesbury, 1st baron, *see* Harris, James
PRO 30/66	Mance, Brigadier General Sir H Osborne, 1899-1924
FO 800/227-228	McNeil, Ronald, 1st baron Cushenden, 1922-1923, 1927- 1929
FO 800/220 FO 794/6B	Mendl, Sir Charles, 1920, 1924, 1926
	Middleton, 1st earl, *see* Brodrick, William
PRO 30/30, FO 848	Milner, Sir Alfred, viscount Milner, 1915-1920
PRO 30/6	Molyneux, Henry Howard, 4th earl of Carnarvon, 1851-1898
FO 800/628-661	Morrison, Herbert, 1951
PRO 30/42	Nicoll, Sir John, 1787-1808
FO 800/336-381, PRO 30/81	Nicolson, Sir Arthur, 1889-1916, 1893-1908
FO 800/249	Noel Baker, Phillip, 1918-1919
	Norwich, 1st viscount, *see* Cooper, Alfred Duff
FO 800/627	Nutting, Anthony, 1953-1955
FO 800/252-254	Oliphant, Sir Lancelot, 1921-1928

FO 354	Parish, Woodbine, 1813-1855
FO 800/233-34	Pelly, Sir Lewis 1859-1863
FO 334	Pierrepont, Sir Henry 1791-1807
FO 323/7	Pigott, Sir Francis, 1884-1887
FO 800/227	Ponsonby, Arthur, 1st baron, 1924
FO 800/3	Ponsonby, Major General Sir Henry, 1870-1894
FO 705	Pottinger, Sir Henry, 1797-1879
	Reading, Marquess of, *see* Isaacs, Rufus
FO 800/304-308	Runciman, Walter, 1938
PRO 30/22	Russell, Lord John, Earl Russell and viscount Amberley, c.1800-1878
FO 918	Russell, Odo, 1st Lord Ampthill, 1851-1887
FO 800/240	Ryan, Sir Andrew, 1881-1928
	Salisbury, 5th Marquess, *see* Gascoyne-Cecil, Robert
FO 800/21	Sanderson, Sir Percy, 1876-1908
FO 800/1-2	Sanderson, Thomas, 1st baron, 1860-1922
FO 800/272-279	Sargent, Sir Orme, 1926-1948
PRO 30/33	Satow, Sir Ernest, 1856-1927
	Scarsdale, 5th baron, *see* Curzon, George
	Sherfield, 1st baron, *see* Makins, Roger
FO 800/285-291	Simon, Sir John, 1931-1935

FO 358	Simmons, General Sir John, 1850-1896
FO 800/241-242, FO 794/5	Spring-Rice, Sir Cecil Arthur, 1903-1918
	Stockton, 1st earl, *see* Macmillan, Harold
FO 342	Stuart de Rothsay, Sir Charles, 1801-1814
PRO 30/36	Stuart, Sir William, 1862-1884
FO 800/221	Sykes, Sir Mark, 1918
	Tenterden, 3rd baron, *see* Charles Abbott
	Thame, Lord Bertie of, *see* Bertie, Francis
FO 933/1-92	Thornton, Sir Edward, 1766-1852, with papers 1793, 1803-1835
FO 933/93-117	Thornton, Sir Edward, 1817-1906, with papers 1847, 1862-1863, 1866-1874, 1875-1886
FO 800/430	Toynbee, Arnold Joseph, 1917
FO 800/220	Tyrrell, Sir William, 1924
	Ullswater, 1st Viscount, *see* Lowther, J W
FO 800/32-33	Vambery, Professor A, 1889-1911
FO 800/22-24 PRO 30/81	Villiers, Sir Francis Hyde, 1893-1923
FO 361	Villiers, George William Frederick, 4th baron Hyde, 4th earl of Clarendon, 1867-1870
	Walden, 6th baron, *see* Ellis, Charles Augustus
PRO 30/26/83	Watson, Edward, 1818-1821

FO 519	Wellesley, Colonel Hon. Frederick, 1809-1830, 1871-1879
FO 519	Wellesley, Henry, 1st baron Cowley, c.1733-1864
FO 519	Wellesley, Henry Richard Charles, 2nd baron and 1st earl Cowley, c. 1833-1871
FO 364	White, Sir William, 1857-1891
FO 323/4	Whitworth, Charles, 1st baron, 1802-1803
FO 800/292	Wigram, Ralph, 1932-1936
CAB 127/158	Wilson, Sir Horace, 1938
FO 800/225-226	Wiseman, Sir W, 1918, 1931
FO 800/309-329	Wood, Edward, 3rd viscount Halifax, 1938-1940
FO 323/9	Wynn, Sir Henry Watkin Williams, 1823-1831

Miscellaneous private office papers of Foreign Office officials can also be found in FO 800/329, 382-399, for the period 1915 to 1924, and in FO 794 for the period 1904 to 1942. Some of the latter, described as 'individual' files are described above.

15. Treaties, Commissions and Conferences

15.1 Treaties

Treaties may result from international conferences or smaller gatherings of officials brought together for specific negotiations. Those in the PRO were created mainly as a result of negotiations for alliances, royal marriages, truces, commercial and financial agreements and pacifications. Besides the official treaty there may be accompanying papers, minutes and other records, which resemble the treaty papers in the state papers in purpose and intent.

The formal documents of a treaty are the protocol, or the articles of agreement, and the ratification. The protocol provides the terms of the treaty as agreed between the negotiating parties, and is signed and sealed by plenipotentiaries on both sides. Accompanying documents may include the full powers, or proofs of ability to negotiate, of the plenipotentiary from the other country or countries involved, and sometimes subsidiary documents. The ratification is the formal acceptance of the treaty by the powers involved, and each country provides a copy signed and sealed by the head of state. These copies are then exchanged during the ratification process. The copies held in the PRO, whether in the state papers or Foreign Office classes, are the copies bearing the seals and signatures of the foreign country or countries involved. It should also be noted that in some cases only one type of the documents described above may survive, and that in the modern period there may be certificates of exchanges of ratifications.

Less solemn agreements may be described under another title in the cases of commercial, boundary or navigation negotiations. Here the final agreement of the parties may be described as a convention, an adhesion (to an agreement), or a declaration. There appears to be little discrimination between the terms in their use.

The earliest treaties in the PRO can be found in the classes described in Chapter 2 and section 5.5 up to c. 1780, and mainly consist of enrolled and original copies. In the pre-Tudor period British treaty relations were restricted mainly to European countries, particularly France, Spain, Portugal and the Low Countries. By the sixteenth century these contacts had widened, and continued to do so with the expansion of British trade and empire.

Some eighteenth- and nineteenth-century treaty material can be found in FO 95, which contains treaty papers 1782 to 1837, and in FO 83, which contains some drafts of British ratifications, 1814 to 1946. Some acceptances and accessions to treaties, 1816 to 1841, are in FO 96. Entry books of treaties with the Barbary States in 1836 can be found in FO 95. There are also two series of entry books and ratifications, with the full powers granted to representatives in FO 95. These cover the period c. 1650 to 1800 and 1800 to 1834. It should also be noted that treaties between the British government and African chiefs can be found in FO 84 and FO 2.

The main classes for modern original treaties are FO 93, which includes the protocols, 1695 to 1989, and FO 94, which includes formal ratifications of treaties, 1782 to 1978. Although FO 93 does contain a few early treaties, the class is at its richest from c. 1800. Treaties up to 1782 are in SP 108. Multilateral treaties, 1907 to 1983, can be found in FO 949, with European Commission treaties, 1953 to 1981, in FO 974. Some conventions can also be found in the modern political correspondence of the Foreign Office.

Warrants under the signature and seal of the sovereign for the great seal to be used in the ratification of full powers, and instruments of consular conventions and agreements can be found in the class C 187. These warrants are countersigned by the foreign secretary and cover the date range 1859 to 1985, although the coverage by year is not continuous.

Besides the treaties themselves and the associated papers there are also documents concerning the process of negotiation of treaties, including memoranda and correspondence. These often include valuable background information. Before 1906 the correspondence of the Treaty Department, which was concerned with the mechanics of negotiation, is to be found intermingled in the individual country classes, although from 1883 such papers may be bound separately within the individual class. There are also some associated papers in FO 83. After 1906 the correspondence of the Treaty Department is contained in a general class, FO 372 (see above, Chapter 12). Some entry books of correspondence relating to treaties have survived in FO 95, FO 96, FO 91 and FO 53.

15.2 Commissions

The composition and purpose of commissions can vary enormously, ranging from a small, temporary investigation to the large scale activities of the Control Commission for Germany, which although technically a commission was in effect an occupying administration of a former enemy state. Commissions can involve representatives from a number of states or may consist of representatives from only two. Negotiations concerning administrative geographical matters may extend over a considerable number of years. The PRO contains records of a number of miscellaneous commissions, including bilateral and multilateral commissions in which Britain took part, mainly as a result of international treaty.

The records of commissions are listed in detail in the *Records of the Foreign Office, 1782-1939*. Records of commissions held in Foreign Office classes mainly concern the slave trade, boundaries, trade and finance, commerce and fishing rights, prizes, claims, reparations and arbitral commissions formed at the end of the First World War. Some of the most important are as follows:

North and South America:

The PRO holds the records of a number of commissions established to deal with Anglo-American claims after the wars of independence, the Anglo-American War of of 1812 and with disputed fishing rights.

FO 301	Archives of the American Fisheries Commission (Washington and Halifax, 1873-1888)
FO 302	Archives of the American North West Boundary Commission, 1872-1876
FO 303	Archives of American Treaty of Ghent Commission, 1796-1829
FO 304	Archives of American Claims Commission, 1794 (1796-1812) See also FO 95.
FO 305	Archives of British and American Claims Commission, 1871 (1871-1875)

FO 306	Archives of British and Brazilian Claims Commission, 1858-1877
FO 307	Archives of British and Buenos Airean Claims Commission, 1831-1834
FO 310	Archives of British and Venezuelan Claims Commission, 1903
FO 317	Register, Commission of Washington, 1871
FO 318	Archives of British and Mexican Mixed Commission, 1866, (1835-1867)
FO 319	Archives of British and Mexican Mixed Commission, 1886, (1885-1889)

Europe:

Many commissions have been formed to deal with issues arising as a result of war and peace treaties. Among the classes listed below, the Eastern Roumelia Commission was formed to guide the creation of an autonomous state as laid down in the Treaty of Berlin in 1878, while the 1840 British and Portuguese Commission was established to investigate the claims of British subjects who had fought during the Portuguese war of liberation. The Archangel Commission was established to organise military assistance to the white Russian and anti-Bolshevik forces in North Russia. After the First World War a number of international commissions were formed to put into effect the various treaties signed with the defeated central powers: the Austrian Inter-Allied Commission of Control was created to administer the disarmament clauses of the Treaty of St Germain, while the Klagenfurt Commission was also established under the terms of that treaty. Britain was represented in the Inter-Allied High Commission for the Rhineland as created under the Treaty of Versailles and the commissions to administer the Schleswig and Upper Silesia regions and plebiscites.

FO 96	Serbian Boundary Commission, 1878-1880
FO 175	Archives of Archangel Allied High Commission, Correspondence (1918-1919, with registers in FO 176)

FO 309	Archives of British and Portuguese Claims Commission 1840, (1840-1849)
FO 311	Archives of Paris Exhibition Commission, 1900 (1897-1901)
FO 316	Archives of Spanish Claims Commissions, 1823 and 1828 (1790-1833)
FO 320	Archives of Albania International Commission of Control (British Delegation), 1913-1914
FO 538	Archives of the Vladivostok Allied High Commission (1818-1921)
FO 852	Archives of the International Plebiscite Commission in Schleswig (1919-1921)
FO 890	Archives of the Inter-Allied Administrative and Plebiscite Commission in Upper Silesia, 1920-1922
FO 894	Archives of Inter-Allied Rhineland High Commission 1920-1930
FO 895	Archives of Klagenfurt Plebiscite Commission, Austria (British Section), 1920
FO 896	Archives of the-Inter Allied Commission of Control in Austria, 1926-1928
FO 901	Archives of Eastern Roumelia Commission, 1878-1879
FO 919	Inter-Governmental Committee on Refugees, Evian, 1938
FO 1017	United Kingdom Delegation for the International Commission for the Ruhr (1949-1951)
FO 1079	European Advisory Commission, 1943-1945. Created to make recommendations on surrender and post war policy after the Moscow conference of 1943.
FO 1086	Austrian Treaty Commission, 1947

FO 1086   Commission of Investigation into former Italian Colonies, 1947-1948

Middle East:

PRO 30/78   Anglo-American Committee on Palestine, 1945 (1945-1947)

Mixed Arbitral Tribunals:

Many tribunals were established after the First World War under various articles of the Peace Treaties.

FO 324   Archives of Anglo-Austrian Mixed Arbitral Tribunal (1921-1930)

FO 325   Archives of Anglo-Bulgarian Mixed Arbitral Tribunal (1921-1927)

FO 326   Archives of Anglo-German Mixed Arbitral Tribunal (1920-1931)

FO 327   Archives of Anglo-Hungarian Mixed Arbitral Tribunal (1921-1931)

FO 328   Archives of Mixed Arbitral Tribunals, Clause 4 Arbitrations (as under clause 4 of annex to various articles of Treaties of Versailles, St Germain and Trianon), 1922-1930

FO 897   Archives of Anglo-American Pecuniary Claims Mixed Arbitral Tribunal (1896-1923)

Slave Trade:

Various commissions were established as a result of the signature of treaties on the slave trade, which were designed to put into effect the agreements reached by the parties.

FO 96   Slave Trade Commission to Zanzibar, 1872-1873 (Sir Bartle Frere)

FO 308	Archives of London Slave Trade Commission, 1819-1824
FO 312	Archives of Cape Town Slave Trade Commission, 1843-1870
FO 313	Archives of Havana Slave Trade Commission, 1819-1869
FO 314	Archives of Jamaica Slave Trade Commission, 1843-1851
FO 315	Archives of Sierra Leone Slave Trade Commission, 1819-1868
FO 317	Commission to revise Instructions to British Naval Officers engaged in Suppression of the Slave Trade, 1881-1882

Compensation and Reparations:

The Reparations Commission was established by the Treaty of Versailles to plan a timetable for German payments for damages caused during the war. By 1924 its work had been overtaken by the Dawes plan. In 1950 the Foreign Compensation Commission was created to investigate claims for loss of property or damages abroad during the Second World War. It dealt mainly with sums granted by foreign countries in agreement with Britain which were to be used for compensation of individuals and businesses.

FO 801 T 194	Archives of the Reparations Commission, 1919 (1919-1931)
FO 1004	Foreign Compensation Commission (1948-1981)

In the state papers there are also similar records, for example the records of the Commissioners for German demands, 1755-1763, in SP 81 and SP 109. Other records of commissions can be found in T 78 (French, Danish and Spanish claims, 1787-1855), T 75 (Surinam Absentees Sequestered Property Commission, 1813-1822), and WO 144 (Inter-Allied Armistice Commission, 1918-1920).

The Control Office for Germany and Austria, the Control Commission for Germany (British Element) and the Allied Commission for Austria (British Element):

Records of the Control Office for Germany and Austria and the British Elements of the Control Commissions for Germany and Austria can also be found amongst the

Foreign Office records. The Control Office, established in London in October 1945 for further planning and administration of the Control Commissions, was eventually incorporated into the Foreign Office in 1947 as the German Division of the Foreign Office. The ministerial head of the Office was initially the chancellor of the Duchy of Lancaster; after 1947 it was the foreign secretary. The activities of the Office and Commission were not just military, but also political, economic and social. Intelligence and information work also became part of the Control Office and Control Commission's duties after the closing of the Political Intelligence Department. The main classes of records for the Control Office are FO 935 to FO 946 inclusive, which contain records of the departments, some private office papers, and records of the central secretariat and the Intelligence Objectives Sub-Committees.

The administration of the British zone was carried out by military and civil bodies in Germany ultimately under the control of the Allied High Commission. The organisation of the Control Commission changed rapidly during the occupation period, but in general a divisional structure was maintained. The records of the Control Commission are arranged by the various divisions or branches created (local and central), and include in addition private papers, records of the central secretariat and the military headquarters. The main classes of records of the Control Commission for Germany (British Element) are as follows: FO 1005 to F0 1006, FO 1008, FO 1012 to FO 1014, FO 1023 to FO 1039, FO 1046 to FO 1047, FO 1049 to FO 1052, FO 1056 to FO 1058, FO 1060 to FO 1078, FO 1082. These classes contain records of the various central and regional bodies established in the British administered zone of Germany, with material spanning 1941 to 1959 in some cases. Subjects covered by these files include military policy, denazification measures, economic conditions and Anglo-American liaison.

Records of the Allied Commission for Austria are in FO 1007 and FO 1020, covering the period 1944 to 1955. FO 1007 contains Library material which is very varied in content, and FO 1020 includes the headquarters and regional files of the Commission.

Further details of these records can be found in parts 1 and 2 of the *Current Guide*. An indexed catalogue to these records has also been published by the German Historical Institute in 1993: *The Control Commission for Germany British Element: Inventory 1945-1955*, by Adolf M Birke, Han Booms and Otto Merker, eds, in 11 volumes. A copy of this work is available in the Reference Room at Kew.

Further material on British policy towards Germany can also be found in the general correspondence in FO 371 and in relevant Cabinet records.

Readers searching for papers relating to a particular commission should also use the index volumes of the *Current Guide*, Part 3, which also include references to records of foreign commissions held in other classes besides those of the Foreign Office, and the 'FO index' volume among the Foreign Office class lists.

The material relating to commissions may also be supplemented by consulting the general correspondence in FO 371 or the general country correspondence classes for the period before 1906. There may also be case volumes relating to a particular commission which collect together all the relevant documentation into a series. (See section 18.2 for further information on cases).

15.3 Conferences

Records which were produced as a result of British involvement in international conferences are spread through a number of classes, not all of them Foreign Office, as many twentieth-century conferences involve heads of state and chiefs of the armed forces as well as diplomatic representatives. Additional material can therefore be found in the records of the War Office, the Admiralty, the Air Ministry, the Ministry of Defence, the Cabinet Office and the Prime Minister's Office. For further details of relevant classes reference should be made to the *Current Guide*.

The documents produced are of a varied nature. They can include formal papers, memoranda and other planning papers, and correspondence between the delegates and the Foreign Office if the conference has taken place abroad. Besides material in Foreign Office files, there may be correspondence in the private office papers of the Prime Minister, in cabinet papers and occasionally references in the embassy and consular archives.

It is also worth bearing in mind that papers touching on international conferences may survive amongst the papers of former diplomats and politicians. Readers should consult the National Register of Archives at the Historical Manuscripts Commission for details of location (for address see p 12).

Records of Conferences are listed in the index to the *Current Guide*, and in the appendix sections of the *The Records of the Foreign Office*. Some of the most important records of conferences are in the following classes:

FO 139	Aix-la-Chapelle, 1818
PRO 30/11	Amiens, 1801-1802
FO 1086	Berlin, 1954
FO 1086	Council of Foreign Ministers (London 1945, Paris 1946, New York 1946, Moscow 1947, London, 1947, Paris 1948, 1949)
FO 1086	Geneva, heads of government, 1955
CAB 31	Genoa, 1923
PRO 30/44/15	The Hague, 1899
FO 840, CAB 29	The Hague, 1920, 1922,1929-1930
FO 839, CAB 29	Lausanne, 1922-1923
FO 840	Locarno, 1925
CAB 29	London, reparations, 1924
CAB 29	London Naval Conference, 1930, 1935-1936
CAB 29	London Conference on Danubian States, 1932
CAB 99	Moscow, 1941
FO 139	Paris, 1814-1815
FO 373, FO 374, FO 608, FO 893, CAB 29	Paris, 1919-1920

FO 1086	Paris, 1954
FO 934	Potsdam, 1945
FO 961	United Nations, 1946-1950
FO 139	Vienna, 1814-1815
FO 139	Verona, 1822
CAB 30	Washington, 1921-1922

Wartime:

CAB 25, CAB 28, CAB 29	First World War (Including Council of Four Heads of Government 1919; Heads of Delegations of the Five Powers 1919; Peace Conferences and Committees, 1919-1922).
CAB 99	Second World War (including Moscow, 1941, all Washington Conferences, Quebec, 1943, 1944, Casablanca, Malta, Cairo, and Teheran, 1943, Yalta 1945, and Berlin/Potsdam 1945).
FO 976	San Francisco Conference, 1945 (establishing the United Nations).

Besides the documents listed above, CAB 133 includes records of international conferences from 1945, and PREM 1, PREM 3, PREM 4, PREM 8 and PREM 11 also include details of British delegations, planning for conferences, foreign visits of the Prime Minister and talks with foreign ambassadors from 1914. For the twentieth century supplementary material can be found in FO 371 and FO 372, FO 800, FO 961, CAB 25, CAB 29 to CAB 31, and CAB 133. Records of delegates and their participation in conferences before 1906 can be found in the case volumes of the country classes of general correspondence.

16. Miscellaneous Sources

There are a number of Foreign Office classes, or parts of a particular class, which cannot be conveniently described under a general heading, yet which provide important information. Some of the most significant are as follows:

16.1 The Chief Clerk's Department

These records, which can be found in FO 366, provide a variety of detail concerning the internal administration of the Foreign Office from the late eighteenth century. After 1782 the Chief Clerk of the old Northern Department became the Chief Clerk of the new Foreign Office. He was not concerned with diplomatic business, except briefly from 1794 to 1824, and despite various changes in the name of the department, has retained general oversight of establishments, personnel, accommodation and finance. During the course of the nineteenth century a number of other functions were brought within the Chief Clerk's department. Between 1841 and 1854 the department also included the Treaty and Royal Letter Department, whose papers for this period can be found here. From 1846 the department also dealt with diplomatic privilege and protocol. In 1854 the treaty and royal letter work was lost, but responsibility for the messenger service was taken over from the Library until 1921. As a result this class includes details of establishments of embassies and consulates abroad, accommodation, personnel policy, communications and messengers, 1854 to 1921, and costs and financing of the Foreign Office and Foreign Service. In the twentieth century a number of internal reforms of the Foreign Office and the diplomatic and consular services were carried out. Papers concerning various internal reforms and reorganisations are also available in this class which also includes the papers of Sir George Rendel, touching on the wartime reform of the Foreign Service, 1941 to 1942.

There are registers of correspondence for the Chief Clerk's archives covering 1868 to 1905, but they do not correspond with the current volume arrangement and are of limited value. References to the Chief Clerk's archives do not appear in the other Foreign Office registers and card indexes before 1919. After this date the contemporary indexing of the papers remains haphazard.

Other establishment and administration records can be found in FO 83, FO 95, FO 96 and FO 900. Entry books containing some warrants and licences for entry into the diplomatic and consular services amongst others, can be found in the Home Office papers in HO 38, covering 1782 to 1969, and HO 37, 1777 to 1863. Some exequaturs, or recognitions of consular officials, are recorded in entry books in HO 43, HO 136 and HO 168. FO 83 contains official letters relating to diplomatic protocol, including credentials, recredentials, and sign manual instructions, including drafts and originals, from 1834 to 1929. FO 83 also includes drafts of full powers to commissioners, 1813 to 1942, drafts to commercial secretaries, 1862 to 1929, and entry books of consular commissions and exequaturs, 1816 to 1929. Some original full powers granted to commissioners can also be found in FO 96 and FO 528.

FO 366 does not provide case files or career details of individual members of the diplomatic service. Sometimes details of individuals are given, where posting or remuneration involved a point of precedent, and some names are mentioned in relation to recruitment policy. There are many references to individual women applicants during the consideration of the admission of women to the unified service from 1941 to 1947.

When tracing the career of an individual it is easiest to start with a systematic survey of the Foreign Office *Diplomatic Lists* from 1854 which are indexed by name and which can be used to establish career progression. The lists do not give any personal details and personal files of members of the service have not been kept.

Superannuation and retirement allowances awarded to members of the diplomatic service are recorded in payment registers in PMG 28. These registers contain payments made to many government officials, diplomats and consular officials being mentioned from c. 1835 to 1932. From 1870 the registers are divided into departmental cuts and are name indexed. The information provided includes the name of the recipient, late office, age on retirement, period of service, salary on retirement and yearly allowance granted, cause of retirement, and occasionally notes of the date of death of the recipient and payments to widows. In the earlier registers addresses of relatives or assignees may be given.

16.2 The Passport Office

Up to 1891 the Chief Clerk was responsible for the issue of passports on behalf of the secretary of state. After this date responsibility passed to the Treaty Department, although the actual duties were performed by a separate office from 1855. After the First World War, regional offices for the issuing of passports were formed, as well as a Passport Control Department, which were designed to meet the great upsurge in demand. The Passport Control Department and its offices abroad also acted in the interwar and war period as a front for intelligence activity, although very few clues to this are provided in the surviving material.

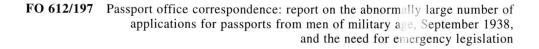

Copy

MINUTE SHEET.   *Reference*

I think it my duty to report that during the last few days we have been receiving a large and abnormal number of applications for passports and endorsements from young men of military age most of whom wish to leave urgently for the United States of America or South America. In cases of established business urgency we are issuing the passports but in others where no such urgency is established we are falling back on the regulations which state that four days notice is required.

In the event of War I assume that some emergency legislation would be passed prohibiting men of military age from leaving the country, in which case I hope the Passport Office will receive early instructions.

17th September, 1938.

FO 612/197   Passport office correspondence: report on the abnormally large number of applications for passports from men of military age, September 1938, and the need for emergency legislation

Early entry books of passes and passports can be found amongst the state papers in SP 44, State Papers Domestic, Entry Books. The correspondence of the Passport Office from 1815 to 1905 and from 1920 onwards can be found in FO 612, with a gap between 1906 to 1919. The correspondence in FO 612 is very varied with files on such subjects as theatrical tours abroad and questions of visas and nationality. Registers for the papers in this class are in FO 613 for 1868 to 1893 and 1898 to 1905. Selective case papers are in FO 737 (for 1916 to 1983) and FO 971 (for the years 1920 to 1969). Passport registers, covering 1795 to 1948, can be found in FO 610, with indexes in FO 611, for the years 1815 to 1916 with gaps between 1863 and 1873. These registers show the intended destination of the applicant. Specimens of passports, 1802 to 1961, are held in the class FO 655, and instructions and order books in FO 948. (The books in FO 948 cover 1983 and are closed for 75 years). Some miscellaneous records can also be found in the papers of the chief clerk, in FO 366. Passport Office correspondence with embassies and consulates, 1886 to 1900, can also be found in FO 614. Early passports issued by embassies or consulates may also be found in the individual embassy and consular correspondence class for the country concerned.

Passport records are described in more detail in PRO *Records Information Leaflet No. 69, Passport Records*. Although they provide useful additional genealogical information, it is worth noting that before the First World War most ordinary travellers did not have passports.

16.3 Royal Letters

Royal letters tend to be of two types: formal documents relating to royal families and heads of state, for example notifications of births, marriages and deaths; and papers concerning formal diplomatic procedures and protocol, for example the issuing of credentials and recredentials, letters of recall, commissions and full powers granted to representatives.

To some extent this material follows on directly from that in the state papers, but after 1782 it is scattered through a number of Foreign Office classes. Royal letters dealing with mainly family affairs can be found in FO 95 which continue to 1930. Case volumes relating to royal family affairs are in FO 83.

Entry books of royal letters were kept amongst the state papers. Some of these can now be found amongst the Foreign Office records, although the distinction from the state paper series is artificial. FO 90 contains a series of entry books which start in 1710, and are arranged by country. From 1828 to 1834 these books are continued in FO 95.

16.4 Confidential Print

From the early nineteenth century (c. 1829), important papers and correspondence on particular subjects were printed for circulation to staff in the Foreign Office, the Cabinet, other government departments and for staff in legations and consulates abroad. The earliest prints appear to have been made of orders in council, texts of treaties and consular notifications. The prints could concern events in a particular country or a specific subject. It is still not entirely clear what prompted the printing of documents for circulation but one explanation is that it was a response to the increasing number of despatches and the need to provide manageable summaries of information.

The prints were numbered individually, in the order of printing. A set of prints arranged by number can be found in FO 881, but there are also classes of confidential prints for particular areas, countries or subjects. A print number can refer to an individual printed document of one page or to many. Copies of confidential print may also be found in the Foreign Office correspondence classes, in embassy and consular archives, private collections and some Cabinet record classes.

One of the most important classes of Confidential Print is FO 881, which contains an almost complete series of confidential prints, covering 1827 to 1914. Much of the confidential print appears to have been destroyed by the Foreign Office in an effort to control the amount of material kept. The series in FO 881 supplements and overlaps with material in the subject and geographical classes up to 1914. From 1914 the confidential print is more likely to be arranged by geographical area, country or by subject, for example, Confidential Print Central Europe, 1920 to 1947 (FO 404), Confidential Print Russia and Soviet Union, 1821 to 1956 (FO 418) and Confidential Print Cultural Propaganda, 1919 to 1938 (FO 431). After 1947 the confidential print is arranged on a country basis. Usually the confidential print is subject to a 50 year closure period.

For a list of Confidential Print classes arranged by geographical area see section 802.9.2 of part 1 of the *Current Guide*. Confidential print can also be identified using the FO index.

27

It is our desire that this committee, once it is set up, should work with as great despatch as possible. It will, we believe, conduce to that result if the committee is no larger than absolutely necessary. Moreover, my colleagues will, I know, appreciate that it is the air Powers who have inevitably specialised knowledge of the difficulties and complexities of the problem, and by whom the consequent action, if any, must be taken.

Nor will the General Commission overlook the fact that it will not, of course, be for this committee to take decisions; that responsibility will rest as always with the General Commission, and every country here represented will share this responsibility when we are in the possession of the results of the work which this committee will do. The suggestion of the committee of air Powers is, therefore, only made because we believe that it will best serve the purpose. Perhaps I should add that the fact that the terms of reference follow closely the terms of the first part of the air proposals contained in the British programme of work must not be taken as meaning that the second part of these proposals dealing with qualitative and quantitative disarmament is now abandoned. That is not so.

One other word as to the composition of the committee. If the General Commission could agree to set up a committee with some such terms of reference as I have proposed, it is not our idea that the committee should be composed of technical experts. On the contrary, I feel confident that we shall more effectively emphasise the importance we attach to the work of this committee, as well as the more certainly further the progress of that work, if we can pay it the compliment of appointing members of the Governments concerned to serve upon it.

I believe that there are one or two members of this General Commission who would prefer that we should take the decision as to the desirability of abolishing naval and military aircraft before we know the results of the work which this committee will do. Though, as an Englishman, I am always timid in an international assembly of pronouncing upon the logical order of events, I am myself confident that we should not do that, but that we should first set up this committee, make it as authoritative as we can, help it to reach its conclusions as speedily as possible, and with the greater certainty and justice we can then ourselves take the decisions that we think fit.

February 16, 1933.

[F 1127/33/10]   No. 10.

APPEAL OF THE CHINESE GOVERNMENT.

DRAFT OF THE REPORT PROVIDED FOR IN ARTICLE 15, PARAGRAPH 4, OF THE COVENANT.

(Communicated by Secretary-General.—Received in Foreign Office, February 20.)

Letter from the President of the Assembly to the Secretary-General.

(Translation.)   *February 15, 1933.*

THE Special Committee of the Assembly (Committee of Nineteen) has found that, after endeavouring, in accordance with the task entrusted to it, to prepare the settlement of the dispute in agreement with the parties, it was unable to make any proposals to the Assembly to this effect. The efforts made with this end in view since the Assembly adopted its resolution of the 9th December last are described in Part II (Section 15) of the attached draft report.

This draft has been prepared by the Committee of Nineteen in execution of the task entrusted to it by Part III (paragraph 5) of the Assembly resolution of the 11th March, 1932, under which the Committee, exercising its functions on behalf of and under the supervision of the Assembly, was instructed to prepare, if need be, the draft of the report provided for in article 15, paragraph 4, of the Covenant.

I should be glad if you would circulate this draft report to the Members of the Assembly, and inform them that, in virtue of the powers conferred on me by the last paragraph of the said resolution of the 11th March, I request the Assembly to meet at Geneva on Tuesday, the 21st February, 1933, at 3·30 P.M.

(Signed)   PAUL HYMANS,
                  President of the Assembly.

FO 411/16   Confidential print, league of Nations: reports on events in the Far East and the results of the enquiry of the Special Committee of the Assembly into Japanese aggression against China, February 1933

16.5 Wartime Departments and Special Functions

During both world wars special departments were created for the execution of various wartime activities. Some of the records of the most important are listed below:

First World War:

FO 882   Arab Bureau, 1911-1920

The Arab Bureau was established in 1916 to co-ordinate British policy in the Near East, and to keep the Foreign, India and War Offices, Indian government and Admiralty informed on German and Turkish policy. It also acted as an intelligence centre and used native agents to incite anti-German demonstrations, and worked closely with the Jeddah Agency. Included are reports from agents, correspondence concerning the revolt in the Hejaz and the activities of T E Lawrence, reports on operations and a series of Arab bulletins, 1916 to 1919.

FO 382   Contraband, 1914-1916

Records of the Ministry of Blockade and the Contraband department, which dealt with the Blockade rather than the Commercial Department, can be found in FO 382. The records are arranged by country or region and by subject, for example there are file series on coal and tonnage and censorship. The files are identical in format to the general correspondence files and contain memoranda and reports and incoming correspondence from other departments concerned in economic warfare and the imposition of the blockade. In 1916 the Contraband Department became the Ministry of Blockade. The indexes and registers described in Chapter 17 and section 18.4 can be used with these records.

FO 833   Foreign Trade Department, 1916-1919

This department was part of the Ministry of Blockade. The records are mainly reports on the formation of the department, black list policy and registers.

FO 686   Jeddah Agency Papers, 1913-1925

The Jeddah Agency was created in 1914. It worked closely with the Arab Bureau (see above) and had paramilitary functions (including a British military mission by 1917). It continued to exist until 1922. Its records refer to tribal and military operations, boundaries and conditions in the Hejaz (including railways and finance), and capitulations. There are also papers on the Arab chiefs, the Sherif of Mecca and Ibn Saud. Correspondence of the High Commissioner, from 1918 to 1919, can also be found. The Agency was linked to the consulate in 1922 and came under Foreign Office control. There is a single set of the consular returns of births, marriages and deaths, 1922 to 1924.

FO 382, FO 845, FO 902   Ministry of Blockade, 1916

The Ministry of Blockade came within the general jurisdiction of the Foreign Office and was created in 1916. Its work was carried out independently, through a number of departments including the War Trade Intelligence Department and War Trade Statistical Department.

FO 371   Political Intelligence Department, 1918-1920

This department was associated with the News Department after 1918. Its function was to collect information from belligerent countries or areas where representation was no longer possible.

FO 383   Prisoners of War and Aliens, 1915-1919

A department to deal with prisoners of war and aliens on a inter-departmental basis was created in 1915. Its records can be referred to using the card indexes and registers described in Chapter 17 and section 18.4.

FO 372   Prize Court Department 1914-1920

This department took over the functions of the Treaty Department in Prize matters during the First World War. The indexes and registers described in Chapter 17 and section 18.4 can be used with these records.

FO 845   Restriction of Enemy Supplies Department, 1916-1919

This department also formed part of the Ministry of Blockade. The records concern agreements between British and foreign governments on export policy, 1916 to 1919. Most of the agreements are with Scandinavian or northern European countries.

FO 902   War Trade Department

See under War Trade Intelligence department.

FO 902, TS 14 War Trade Intelligence Department

In 1916 the War Trade Intelligence Department of the Ministry of Blockade was established. It was responsible for the collection, collation and distribution of trade and economic intelligence in general. Its records include reports on firms, cargoes, contraband, black lists and publications, (mainly weekly bulletins) and summaries of blockade information, 1915 to 1919 (in FO 902). Those in TS 14 (held at Chancery Lane) are minutes of meetings of the Contraband Committee, the General Black List Committee and the Enemy Export Committee. Also included are war trade statistics for Scandinavia, the Netherlands and Switzerland, 1915, 1917, 1918 and 1919.

FO 371 War Department (Eastern and Western Political Departments), 1914-1920

The War Department was formed from the amalgamation of these two peacetime departments. It dealt with diplomatic and political aspects of the war as well as military and naval matters. Its records form part of the general correspondence of the Foreign Office political departments and can be traced using the card indexes and registers described in Chapter 17 and section 18.4.

Second World War:

During the Second World War the Central Department of the Foreign Office became the General or War Department, with responsibilities for governments in exile. Other departments, for example the French Department, were also created. Files for these departments can be found in FO 371.

FO 957   British Middle East Office, 1946

This office succeeded the Middle East Supply Centre, and continued its work in providing advice on social and economic development policy for British territories in the area. Files relating to its work, 1946 to 1983, cover such topics as regional economic policy, railways, irrigation, land reclamation, public health and forestry development. In July 1961 it was renamed the Middle Eastern Development Division and became part of the newly formed Department of Technical Co-operation.

FO 115   British Purchasing Agency (USA), 1939

Files on the organisation and establishment of the Agency can be found in this class. It also includes reports on American economic capacity, British commodity needs and transport arrangements between the two countries.

FO 115   British Purchasing Commission (USA), 1939-1940

Also included in FO 115 are files on the reorganisation of the existing administration, co-ordination with other purchasing agencies, and British supply needs (aircraft, explosives, food, chemicals and machines, amongst others).

FO 115   British Supply Council in North America, 1941-1944

Similar files on supplies and British requirements under Lend-lease arrangements can be found in FO 115. Also included are records of the British Raw Materials Mission. See also CAB 115.

FO 660, FO 892   British Mission to the French National Committee, 1940-1943

The French National Committee was established in London in 1941 and a British Mission was appointed to it for liaison purposes. By 1943, after the invasion of North Africa, the French authorities in Africa joined with the Committee to form the French Committee of National Liberation. British Mission records include those of the Minister Resident at Allied Force headquarters, Algiers, 1943 (Harold Macmillan) and the United Kingdom Representative with the French Committee of National Liberation at Algiers, 1943 to 1944 (Duff Cooper). Records of the British mission can also be found in FO 892. These files cover various aspects of Anglo-French relations, attitudes to General de Gaulle, Franco-American relations and the French colonies. Other relevant records can be found in FO 371, FO 921 and FO 922. There are also papers concerning the welfare of French nationals in FO 1055, covering 1940 to 1945.

FO 942, FO 943, FO 1032   Economic and Industrial Planning Staff (Control Office, Germany)

The Economic and Industrial Planning Staff, or EIPS, was established in April 1944. It was responsible for planning economic policy towards Germany, Italy and the Far East. In 1945 its work as regards Germany and Austria passed to the Control Office. Its files are very varied, covering political, economic, financial and constitutional policy towards the occupied territories. The class contains records of wider importance, including some relating to allied control organisations in the Balkan states and peace negotiations with Italy.

FO 922   Middle East Supply Centre, 1941-1945

The Middle East Supply Centre was established at Cairo from 1941 to 1945. Its function was to ensure the free movement of military supplies by the direction and regulation of civil supplies. After the United States' entry into the war it became an Anglo-American organisation. Files covering 1938 to 1945 can be found in this class. They include records of the Director General's Office, the Spears Mission to Syria and Lebanon, and papers on transport, agriculture and industrial production. See also FO 921, MT 59 for related material.

FO 660, FO 921 Ministers Resident, 1942-1945

This class is comprised of files and correspondence of the political liaison officer with the United States forces in Britain and the United Kingdom and North Africa, 1942 to 1943 (W H B Mack); the minister resident at Allied Forces Headquarters, North Africa, 1943 to 1944 (Harold Macmillan) and the United Kingdom representative with the French Committee of National Liberation at Algiers, 1943 to 1944 (Duff Cooper). Files of the office of the Minister of State, Cairo, are in FO 921. They cover the period 1942 to 1946.

FO 837   Ministry of Economic Warfare, 1939-1945

The Ministry was established in September 1939 with the aim of undermining the enemy's economy and its capacity to wage war. It concerned itself with all aspects of economic policy, trade and supply relations with neutrals. The Ministry operated as a cover organisation for the Special Operations Executive but remained separate from it. Its files cover organisation and administration, economic intelligence, blacklisted business firms, minutes of various committees (for example the Blockade Committee, Contraband Committee and Enemy Export Committee), contraband control and pre-emptive purchasing policy, including some files of the United Kingdom Commercial Corporation. Further records relating to the latter are in BT 192 and T 263. The Enemy Branch, or Economic Advisory Branch from 1944, acted as a liaison organisation with the Foreign Office. Its records, mainly concerned with economic intelligence, are in this class. Records of the Economic Warfare Department, which took over many of the Ministry's functions after its demise, are in FO 935.

FO 371, FO 898   Political Intelligence Department, 1939-1946

FO 898 includes some files concerning liaison between the Political Warfare Executive and the Political Intelligence Department. Most of the files relating to its work are in the general political correspondence.

FO 898   Political Warfare Executive, 1941-1946

Files contained in this class cover the administration of the organisation from its formation in 1941, and include records of the central directorate and the regional or country directorates. PWE produced propaganda for all enemy and enemy occupied territories. It worked in co-operation with the Foreign Office, SOE, the Ministry of Information and the BBC amongst others, and was responsible for both 'black' and 'white' propaganda. By 1943 it was also involved in operational planning with the landing of allied troops in Africa and Europe. PWE's records contain many files concerning liaison with other departments (including SOE) and intelligence reports on conditions and morale in Europe. There are file series on propaganda, PWE missions, leaflet policy, involvement with military operations, post-war planning and initial input into the work of the Control Commissions. There are also copies of PWE leaflets and publications.

FO 916   Prisoners of War and Internees, 1940-1946

Records produced by the new Consular (War) Prisoners of War Department are in FO 916. This class includes reports on prisoner of war camps in Germany, Italy and occupied countries in Europe and the Far East, conditions of camps and treatment of prisoners and internees, and the welfare of sick and wounded. There are also files on repatriations, exchanges of prisoners, the activities of the Vatican on behalf of prisoners, the Imperial War Graves Commission and on the liberation of prisoners from the camps. Also included are reports on British internment camps.

War trials:

Most of the Foreign Office files on the war crimes trials were transferred to the Imperial War Museum in 1966. One class of related material is available at the PRO (FO 1019). Other records can be found amongst the War Office classes. FO 371 contains files on the investigation of war criminals, and papers on British involvement in the United Nations War Crimes Commission. Further references to PRO sources for war crimes can be found in Appendix B of *The Second World War: A*

Guide to documents in the Public Record Office, by John Cantwell, (London, HMSO 1993). The Foreign Office records also contain files on the interrogation of Rudolf Hess after his flight to Scotland in May 1941 and other personal papers relating to his captivity. Many documents were captured from enemy archives during the later stages of the war. Copies of German Foreign Ministry documents can be found in the GFM classes at Kew. There are many War Office records relating to war trials and criminals, for example WO 235, WO 309, WO 310, WO 311, WO 325, WO 331, WO 343, WO 356 and WO 357. A fuller description of these records can be found in the following PRO Records Information Leaflets: *War Crimes of the Second World War: Documents in the Public Record Office* (number 85) and *Captured Enemy Documents: Files of the German Foreign Ministry* (number 64).

FO 1019   Nuremburg trials,correspondence and papers, 1934 to 1937

F0 1093   Rudolf Hess, Miscellaneous Unregistered papers, 1941-1945

16.6 Sources in other classes

The conduct of foreign policy, particularly in the modern age, concerns a number of other departments, including those dealing with defence, planning and economic resourcing, all of which factors are taken into account in the formulation of policy at the highest level. For this reason material of relevance can be found amongst the records of the Cabinet and its committees dealing with international policy, the Treasury, the Board of Trade and its successors, the Prime Minister's Office and the modern Ministry of Defence and its predecessors (the Admiralty, the War Office, and the Air Ministry). The records of the British Council (in the BW classes at Kew) provide information on the direction of cultural diplomacy abroad. The records of the Treasury Solicitor (TS classes at Chancery Lane) may include references to legal advice provided in specific international questions. Treasury records are also an important source for international financial policy, as are the records of the Export Credits Guarantee Department (ECG classes). The PRO also holds records of the Department of Technical Co-operation and the Ministry of Overseas Development (the Overseas Development Administration, when part of the FCO) in the OD classes, and records of the modern Foreign and Commonwealth Office created in 1968 (FCO classes). Relatively few records of the FCO have been transferred under the 30 year rule; those that have are mainly colonial government gazettes, although FCO 1 does contain photocopies of documents made available to the Australian Royal Commission on nuclear weapons testing in Australia, 1950 to 1979.

For imperial and colonial policy readers should consult the Colonial Office and Dominions Office records which are described more fully in Public Record Office Handbook no.3, *The Records of the Colonial and Dominions Offices*, by R B Pugh (HMSO 1964, new edition to be published shortly). Records of the Colonial Office are held at the PRO at Kew, as are the records of the Dominions Office, 1925 to 1947. In 1947 the Dominions Office was renamed the Commonwealth Relations Office; its records and that of its predecessor can be found in the DO classes. The Colonial Office and the Commonwealth Relations Office combined in 1966 to become the Commonwealth Office, which in turn combined with the Foreign Office in 1968 to form the Foreign and Commonwealth Office.

Records of the India Office, created in 1858, and its predecessors, can be consulted at the Oriental and India Office Collections of the British Library. These collections also include the records of the Burma Office, from its creation in 1937 to 1948. After Burmese independence in 1948, relations with Britain were dealt with by the Foreign Office as Burma did not join the Commonwealth.

Special Operations Executive records in the process of transfer to the PRO also contain information about the Executive's relations with the Foreign Office. Records of SOE in the Far East in the class HS 1 include correspondence between SOE agents and the Foreign Office on political questions c. 1940 to 1946, while HS 2 contains similar information about Denmark, Norway, Sweden and Britain, c. 1940 to 1946. These records are described in more detail in: Louise Atherton, *SOE Operations in the Far East. An Introductory Guide to the Newly Released Records of the Special Operations Executive in the Public Record Office*, (PRO Publications, 1993) and *SOE Operations in Scandinavia. A Guide to the Newly Released Records in the Public Record Office*, (PRO Publications, 1994). Records of SOE in Africa are expected to be made available shortly.

For further details of relevant classes you should consult the index to the *Current Guide* and the class descriptions in Part 2 before proceeding to the lists.

16.7 Maps and Plans

Maps, plans and atlases accumulated in the Foreign Office Library, dated 1700 to 1940, are in FO 925. This class also contains items collected by diplomats for military, commercial or negotiating purposes and which were incorporated in despatches and reports. The collection also contains maps relating to Africa and colonial areas. Many different types of maps are available, often in a variety of languages. Among the many types covering Europe, Asia and Africa are: statistical, demographic and ethnographical maps; maps illustrating military defences; maps relating to boundary questions, treaties and international demarcations (including fishing rights); Admiralty charts and other maritime maps; plans of buildings, including the Foreign Office, embassies, consulates and other buildings abroad, and maps of steamship routes, telegraph lines and railways. Some maps of the United Kingdom are also available in this class, dated 1715 to 1885. The maps are indexed by a card system which forms part of the class FO 1088, which also includes a series of registers. The topographical card index can be consulted in the Map and Large Document Room, Kew.

Plans of embassies, consulates and legations abroad can be found in WORK 40. Most date from the late nineteenth century to the early twentieth century. Related correspondence can be found in WORK 40 and photographs in WORK 55.

16.8 International bodies and organisations

The Public Record Office does not contain the central archives of organisations such as the League of Nations, the United Nations, the North Atlantic Treaty Organisation (NATO), the Western European Union (WEU), or any of the organisations established by the European Community. The records of the United Nations are held at the UN archives in New York, with a library of documents and UN publications in Geneva. Some League of Nations records are also held at the United Nations Library in New York but most are held at Geneva. European Community records were opened to the public in 1983 (under a 30 year rule) at the Historical Archives of the European Community Commission, Florence. Central NATO records, or those of its predecessor the European Defence Community, are not available for research. However, details of British involvement in most of these organisations can be found in some of the record classes held at the PRO, particularly in the Foreign Office political correspondence (FO 371), prime ministerial papers (PREM classes), Cabinet records (CAB classes) and Ministry of Defence classes (DEFE). Some of the most important of these classes are listed below:

International Committee for the Application of the Agreement regarding Non-Intervention in Spain:

Minutes, memoranda, and sub-committee papers, 1936 to 1939, are in FO 849. See also CAB 62.

League of Nations:

PRO 30/52	Assembly and Council documents, 1920-1946 (comprising records of the London Office of the League, official journals and the papers of D H Boggis-Rolfe, League delegate in investigation of Bulgarian finances, 1933.)
FO 95/803	League of Nations Section, miscellaneous correspondence 1935-1938
CAB 29	League of Nations Monetary and Economic Conference, London, 1933
MAF 40	Agricultural Departments
BT 11	Board of Trade consultation
CO 967	Colonial Office papers
FO 411	Confidential print, 1924-1941
FO 371	Correspondence (League of Nations Department)
FO 800/400	Private Office Papers, 1918-1924

Sources in other classes are described more fully in PRO Records Information Leaflet 76, *Records Relating to the League of Nations.*

United Nations:

FO 371	United Nations Department (Foreign Office)
OD 13, OD 9	United Nations Economic Commission for Africa
BW 79, ED 157, FO 924	United Nations Educational Scientific and Cultural Organisation

FO 961, FO 1084, CAB 142	United Nations UK mission and delegation records
TS 26	United Nations War Crimes Commission
DEFE 12	UN Command (Korea)
FO 472, FO 475, FO 502	United Nations Confidential Print
CAB 142	United Nations Relief and Rehabilitation Administration, UK delegation

North Atlantic Treaty Organisation:

DEFE 7, DEFE 11	Chief of staff files
T 220, T 225, T 229, T 234, T 235	Treasury files

Brussels Treaty Organisations (Western European Union):

DG 1	Agreements, and files relating to the Consultation Council (Microfilm copies, to be seen only on production of authorisation from the WEU in Brussels).

Organisation for European Economic Cooperation (OEEC):

FO 1009	United Kingdom delegation files, 1948-1957
T 232, T 237	Work in the Economic Recovery programme

European Economic Community:

Records relating to British involvement are spread throughout the records - see the index (Part 3) to the *Current Guide*. Many of the papers so far released on the British application to join the community can be found in FO 371, as well as in Cabinet, Treasury and Prime Minister's Office record classes. European treaties can be found in FO 974, and records of the European Economic Co-operation Committee in T 232 and T 235. The actual records of the European Community are in the process of being deposited at the Historical Archives of the European Communities, Villa il Poggiolo, Piazza Edison, 11, I-50133, Florence. They are described in the *Guide to the Historical Archives of the European Comunities,* by Jean Marie Palayfet (Florence, 1993).

International Refugee Organisation:

FO 1084   Records of the United Kingdom permanent delegation and involvement in liquidation, 1953.

Council of Foreign Ministers:

FO 1086   Post-war meetings and decisions, 1945-1955

16.9 Foreign Office Background Briefing Papers

Classes of background historical papers produced by the Foreign Office for the information of officials are also available in the PRO. Some of these have been opened in advance of the thirty-year rule. Although background papers can be found in the files of the political departments, there are also specific classes as follows:

FO 373 Peace Conference of 1919 to 1920 Handbooks

Produced by the Historical Section for the use of officials attending the conference, they cover 1918 to 1919. Most are printed and contain maps, histories, geographical and economic surveys and occasionally extracts from and lists of past treaties.

FO 972 Foreign Policy Documents, 1978-1992

Papers in this class were prepared in the Research Department of the Foreign and Commonwealth Office as background information for officials. Their content is extremely wide ranging and covers international events on a global basis. Some reports on the structure of the FCO and the conduct of British policy are included but the main emphasis is upon the provision of foreign information. The records in this class and in FO 973 (see below) include some of the most modern documents of the FCO which are open to research. Subjects covered include the United Nations, political conditions in particular states, human rights, propaganda, histories of negotiations and reports on treaties and arms control amongst others. Examples include 'Cultural Policy in Poland' (1987) and 'The Diplomatic Service, basic facts and figures 1991-1992' (1992).

FO 973 Background Briefs, 1978-1992

These papers were also prepared by the FCO Research Department. They include general reports on the progress of particular negotiations, regimes, dissidents abroad, demographic trends, refugees, treaties, conferences and economic conditions. Topics such as 'Life Today in Vietnam' (1980) and 'The Falkland Islands: Self-Determination' (1982) appear in these files.

FO 975 Information Reports, 1948-1954

This class contains papers prepared by the Information Research Department for the use of officials overseas. Most are reports on conditions in the USSR and eastern Europe. Subjects covered include Stalinism, communism in eastern bloc countries, human rights, education and youth movements, Soviet foreign policy and communism in China and Indo-China.

May 1982

FALKLAND ISLANDS: SELF-DETERMINATION

That this House wishes it to be conveyed to Her Majesty's Government that the people of the Falkland Islands have shown overwhelmingly that they wish to remain British.

Motion adopted by the Falkland Island Legislative Council, December 1977.

Under the UN Charter, "friendly relations among nations based on respect for the principle of equal rights and self-determination of peoples" (Article 2)) are listed as one of the purposes of the UN. Continued recognition of this fundamental principle constitutes one of the most valuable protections enjoyed by small States and peoples against the encroachment of more powerful States. The United Nations has never countenanced the decolonisation of a territory by agreeing to hand a people over to alien rule in the face of their persistent opposition, and the principal UN Resolution on decolonisation (1514) specifically declares that "all peoples have the right to self-determination; by virtue of that right they freely determine their political status and freely pursue their economic, social and cultural development".

The term "people" sometimes gives difficulties, and no definition has yet been agreed on in the United Nations. The populations of many South American countries are dominated by the descendants of European settlers, the indigenous people having been frequently eliminated. There were no indigenous inhabitants of the Falklands, and the present inhabitants have the same right to be accepted as a "people" as those who live in other South American countries.

On 2 April 1982, the Falkland Islanders' ability to determine their own lives and future was taken from them by force through Argentina's invasion and occupation - an action which was not only a gross violation of the terms of the UN Charter, but also of the 1947 Inter-American Treaty of Reciprocal Assistance (Rio Treaty) whose contracting parties "undertake in their international relations not to resort to the threat or use of force in any manner inconsistent with the provisions of the Charter of the UN". And signatories of the Charter of the Organisation of American States agree to "strengthen the peace and security of the continent" (Article 2) and "bind themselves in their international relations not to have recourse to the use of force" (Article 21).

This paper has been prepared for general briefing purposes. It is not and should not be construed or quoted as an expression of Government policy.

FO 973/241   Foreign Office information: background brief produced in May 1982, 'The Falkland Islands and Self Determination'

111

FO 1059 Information Department: Periodicals 1952-1954

This class contains copies of 'The Interpreter', 1952-1954, which offered guidance on foreign official and newspaper reports, mainly those emanating from communist countries in Europe and the Far East.

16.10 Foreign Office Administration of Territories Overseas

In the post war period the Foreign Office has been directly involved in the administration of territory in Africa and the Far East. Records relating to these duties can be found in the following classes:

Africa:

FO 1015 Foreign Office Administration of African Territories, 1915-1952

After the Second World War Britain administered directly the former Italian colonies of Eritrea, Somalia, Cyrenaica, and Tripolitania. From April 1950 Somalia was administered by Italy under UN trusteeship. Records of the British Resident in Libya during the period of British administration are in FO 1021, while those of the military authorities are in WO 230.

South East Asia:

FO 1091 Commissioner General for the United Kingdom in South East Asia and United Kingdom Commissioner for Singapore and South East Asia, 1950-1961

The records in this class cover a broad geographical area (including the Malayan Union, Sarawak, Singapore and Brunei), and contain information of both colonial and political importance. A number of offices were created to administer the area after the Second World War; the records of two of them are available in this class. The first Commissioner General for the United Kingdom, Malcolm MacDonald, was appointed in May 1948. He continued to exercise the power of the former Governor General, a post created in 1946, over the areas mentioned above. He also took over the role of the Special Commissioner, a diplomatic post created in 1946, which involved providing advice on general policy in an area including Burma, Indo-China and Siam. In these duties the Foreign Secretary continued to have direct oversight. The files in this class relate to these duties and policy in south east Asia generally, including Singapore after 1959, when the office was merged with that of the Commissioner for that region. There are, however, significant gaps in the records available in this class.

17. Registers, Indexes and Means of Reference: 1782-1960

The indexes and registers described in this section are referred to in more detail in Chapter 18, which provides practical guidance in their use.

The organisation of documents relating to foreign affairs into a registration system is a modern development. The state papers were not arranged in a regular manner and although there may be lists and précis of documents in the list of contemporary indexes (IND 1) these rarely key directly to the modern arrangement of the documents although they do provide much information about their previous arrangement. Further guidance on how to use the state papers foreign is given below in section 18.1. Only in the early nineteenth century did the increasing amount of correspondence and papers result in efforts to control incoming and outgoing information. Various forms of filing, registration and indexing were used from c.1810, and these systems now form the basis for locating specific documents, where they have survived and have been transferred to the PRO.

The earliest Foreign Office registers are in FO 95, covering material from c.1782 to 1789 and 1805 to 1810. They appear to have been created to show dates of receipts and issues and were not linked to a filing system. From 1809 each department began to keep a daily record of correspondence in its own registers (the commercial and treaty departments followed suit later). Known later as departmental diaries, these books contain details of incoming and outgoing correspondence, with registration numbers which were docketed onto the incoming papers; registration numbers for outgoing correspondence were introduced later and at varying times. Some early departmental diaries from 1809 to 1818 are also available in FO 95. They continue in FO 566.

The main series of indexes and registers which can be used to locate general correspondence are as follows:

Departmental diaries and registers, 1817-1920 (FO 566)

These indexes and registers were kept on a day to day basis in the departments. Each department had its own style of register, although by the end of the century some uniformity had been achieved. During this period different types of registers were created for the new departments and functions of the Office. This class includes the early diaries, departmental diaries 1817 to 1890, registers used after 1891 up to 1905, which attempted to provide fuller subject details and which have standard abbreviations, and general registers 1906 to 1920. These registers are now arranged by country, with several years' registry details to a single volume, or by department. The nineteenth-century country registers have separate headings for diplomatic, consular, commercial and treaty material. Not all of the nineteenth-century registers have survived however; there are significant gaps in those dealing with the Slave Trade. After 1911 and up to 1920 the registers are arranged by subject type (for example, contraband, commercial, consular) and chronologically by country under a specific country code used by the department.

The registers reflect the political changes of the nineteenth century and can refer to regions, states (for example pre-1871 components of Germany) or to conferences, commissions or subjects (for example the Slave Trade).

New registers were created during the First World War. The general registers were divided into diplomatic and war series. Separate series were created for the Contraband and Prisoners of War Departments. The contraband registers, like the correspondence, are arranged by region or subject.

Library Series of registers and indexes of General Correspondences, 1808-1890 (FO 802/FO 605)

These registers and indexes were created in the Library of the Foreign Office after the general correspondence to which they referred had passed out of current use. These registers are now available to readers as microfilm copies, in the class FO 605 (covering 1761-1893) and refer to papers in the general correspondence between 1808 and 1890 in the general correspondence classes before 1906. They are arranged in order of correspondence with fuller descriptions than those given by the diaries. This means that they are more useful for finding particular papers in the 1809 to 1890 period, and the microfilms in FO 605 should be used in preference to the registers in FO 566 for this period. The registers are compiled by country with separate headings for diplomatic correspondence (also called foreign, embassy or political), consuls, consular domestic, and domestic; (domestic here refers to correspondence with foreign ministers in Britain). The indexes, which refer to the registers rather than the correspondence, are not arranged in strictly alphabetical order. The indexes refer to subjects (including places and ships) and persons, but as they are not invariably accurate they should be used with caution.

Indexes to General Correspondence, 1891-1905 (FO 804/FO 738)

Indexes to material in the FO 566 departmental registers dating from 1891 to 1905 are preserved in these classes. The general, commercial and consular indexes are, on the whole, arranged separately, while the political department indexes are arranged by country or region and refer to persons and subjects. The indexes to the diplomatic country registers are available to the public in the form of photocopies in the class FO 738, available on open access in the Reference Room, Kew. For consular, general and commercial correspondence in the original registers in FO 804 must be ordered.

Numerical (Central) Registers of General Correspondence, 1906-1920 (FO 662)

After 1906, with the creation of a central registry in the Foreign Office, new and more detailed registers of general correspondence were kept on a daily basis. The indexes are in the form of cards, and the original card indexes can be consulted in the Reference Room at Kew. As the new registry system instituted in 1919-1920 was introduced at different times by different departments this card index covers some papers for 1920. A search involving files of 1920 may require use of the card indexes and the printed indexes (see FO 409, below). The references on the cards are not current PRO references and need to be converted. Practical guidance on how to do this is provided in section 18.4.1. Much material covered by the indexes has not survived.

Indexes (Printed Series) to General Correspondence 1920-1951 (FO 409)

After 1920 another system of registration was introduced in the Foreign Office. The indexing of files continued to be in the form of index cards, which have been preserved in the class of Indexes (Printed Series) to General Correspondence (FO 409). These indexes have been reprinted in volume form by the Kraus-Thomson Organisation and can be consulted in the Reference Room at Kew. They cover the period 1921 to 1951. Also included are the 'green indexes' referring to papers in the general correspondence marked under the green file heading denoting confidential or secret papers. Green papers are included in the general index after 1941 (see section 18.4.2).

After 1951 the Foreign Office Registry system changed once again. At the time of writing the PRO has no indexes or registers for the records later than 1951. The only means of reference to the general correspondence after this date is by means of the PRO lists, although there is a PRO listing project in progress for the post-1951 period.

Embassy and consular archives also had their own contemporary systems of registration. Registers of particular consulates are now arranged in separate record classes and can be identified using the FO index which is a separate binder at the start of the FO lists available in the Reference Room at Kew. This index lists classes of embassy and consular material and letter books and registers of correspondence by country. In a country where a large number of consulates were maintained, for example Turkey, each consulate could have its own register of correspondence.

As a general point, registers and indexes should be approached with caution by researchers. The indexes are roughly contemporary to the material as it was produced and used, and many of the documents referred to have been destroyed under departmental review. This means that although an item may appear in the indexes it may not necessarily appear where it ought to be in a file or volume. The lists show complete ranges of file numbers and do not indicate gaps. Often the only way to find if a file has survived is to search through the original document itself. Disappointments can therefore occur.

18. Approaches to Research

18.1 Using the State Papers Foreign

There is no single method of approaching the state papers foreign, simply because the means of reference vary so widely. Finding aids can provide the detail of a calendar, containing individual summaries of documents, or a one line entry in a handlist. Section 6.1 has already described some of the calendars and lists available. However, the best way to use the papers is to begin by identifying which of the record classes in the SP series is most relevant for the subject of enquiry. The most efficient starting point is the index to the *Current Guide*, followed by use of by the class descriptions in Part 2 to obtain a more detailed summary of the contents of a class. Not all classes have yet been described fully in this work so reference should also be made to older guides which are available in the Round Room at Chancery Lane. It should be noted that the state papers foreign can only be consulted at Chancery Lane.

To locate the list for the class or classes identified, readers should use the card index of locations in the Round Room at Chancery Lane which is arranged alphanumerically by lettercode and class number; for example SP 63 will be followed by SP 64 and so on. The card index provides a list of all relevant lists, calendars and other indexes available in the room, giving the location in the following type of format: 1/62. The number 1 refers to the number of the book stack or bay, and the 62 refers to the number of the book on the shelf in the Round Room. Many lists for the state papers foreign classes are now in the new Standard List Set, which are the yellow binders in bays 3 and 4. Those available in this format will be marked in the card index system. From the list readers can identify further references which are needed to order the document using the document ordering terminals.

The calendars provide very detailed means of reference to the records and are particularly useful for the genealogist as they do contain indexes which include names. The document references can usually be extracted from these volumes using the key at the front of the book. Where no calendars or semi-calendars in the form of lists are available speculative searches must be resorted to by the researcher. For surveys of particular periods there is no alternative to detailed sifting of the records which is necessarily time consuming but essential for scholarly coverage. Many of the state papers are arranged in bundles or volumes and identified by the name of the individual secretary of state or diplomat, so it is useful to find out from the works listed in section 4 and the *Handbook of British Chronology* (third edition, Royal Historical Society, 1986) the dates of office of the secretary and officials concerned, the department involved and the geographical arrangement of duties. It is also worth bearing in mind that secretaries of state could make 'local arrangements' in the discharge of their duties, and it is always worth checking the papers arranged under the other secretary of state for the period and country involved.

---

180   FOREIGN PAPERS.

A.D. 1567.
Feb. 23.   **968.**   ROBERT MELVILLE to CECIL.

If the Queen of England would dispatch a gentleman to his mistress it would be well taken of her and do much good at this time. Desires to know what time in the morning he may speak with her Highness. *Signed.*
Add. Endd., with seal. *P.* ¾.

Feb. 23.   **969.**   PIETRO BIZARRI to CECIL.

Sends news from Rome of 15 Feb. 1567 ; and Troppan, 10 Feb.—Venice, 23 Feb. 1567. *Signed.*
Add. Endd., with seal. *Ital. Pp.* 3.

Feb. 24.   **970.**   JOHN BENNET to CECIL.

Has had motion made to him that because he has been lately complained of to have sold to certain pirates the Queen's ordnance and artillery it were not good for him to deny Nicholas Harrington's suit lest a worse thing might chance to him. Has removed by purgation the suggestion concerning the sale, and desires license to come up to require hearing concerning all the premises. *Signed.*
Add. Endd. : 24 Feb. 1566. *P.* 1.

Feb. 24.   **971.**   The QUEEN to MARY QUEEN OF SCOTS.

Is horrified at the abominable murder of her husband. Most people say that she has not looked to the revenge of this deed, nor to touch those who have done it. Exhorts her to show to the world what a noble princess and loyal wife she is. Desires her to ratify the treaty made six or seven years ago.—Westminster, 24 Feb.
Copy. Endd. Fr. P. 1.

Feb. 25.   **972.**   RICHARD FREARSON and others to SIR HENRY NORRIS.

Beg that he will take pity and help them, being twenty-four poor Englishmen taken at Rouen and now in the galleys at Marseilles.—Marseilles, 25 Feb. 1566. *Signed.*
Add. P. 1.

Feb. 26.   **973.**   ROBERT MELVILLE to CECIL.

Desires that the treasurer of the Queen of Scots may have the favour of kissing the Queen's hand. The Queen has gone to Seton to repose. The Earl of Murray is sent for. The Earl of Athol has parted. All the Lords are sent for. The committers of this last fact are not revealed. Parliament is proclaimed for 14th April. The Prince is at Holyrood. *Signed.*
Add. Endd. P. 1.

Feb. 26.   **974.**   SIR THOMAS GRESHAM to CECIL.

Desires that he may have 4,000*l.* or 5,000*l.* by the 1st of April for the better satisfaction of the Queen's credits.—Canterbury, 26 Feb. 1566. *Signed.*
Add. Endd. P. ½.

The Calendar of State Papers Foreign, Elizabeth, 1566-1568, (volume VIII, 1871), showing summaries of documents relating to Anglo-Scottish relations in 1567 and the effects of the murder of Darnley 1567

A.D. 1567.
July 18.   **1468.**   SIR NICHOLAS THROCKMORTON to the QUEEN.

1. Cannot perceive that as yet access to the Queen will be granted to him. Robert Melville returned from the Queen on the 17th, who has written desiring better treatment, and has offered to commit the government wholly to the Earl of Murray, or else to the Duke of Chatelherault and other noblemen. She has written that he may have access to her. She will by no means abandon Bothwell for her husband. She yields to the prosecution of the murder. Has found means to let her know that he has been sent hither for her relief, and has persuaded her to renounce Bothwell. She sends word that she would rather die, taking herself to be seven weeks gone with child, and by renouncing him she would acknowledge herself to be with child of a bastard. Knox arrived on the 17th. Has persuaded with him and Craig to preach leniency. Finds them both very austere in this conference. The Bishop of Galloway assures these Lords that there is a good disposition in the other party to concur with them, and they can be content that the Queen's restraint be continued until the murder be punished. Captain Clerke who served at Newhaven has killed Wilson a seaman, by whose death the enterprise to impeach Bothwell is dashed. The Hamiltons would concur with these Lords in all things in any extremity against the Queen, so that the Earl of Lennox's son should not inherit after the Prince.

2. Though the Lords and counsellors speak reverently and charitably of their Queen, so that he cannot gather from their speech any intention to cruelty or violence, yet he finds that the Queen is in very great peril of her life, by reason that the people mind vehemently her destruction. It is a public speech that she has no more privilege to commit murder and adultery than any private person. Earl Bothwell has been put to the horn. His porter and another servant have confessed that he was one of the principal executors of the murder in his own person accompanied with sundry others. Bothwell is still in the north. These Lords keep the passages from the north and west with their harquebusiers. Of late this Queen has written a letter to the Captain of Dunbar, which being surprised discovers matters little to her advantage. —Edinburgh, 18 July 1567. *Signed.*
    Pp. 4.

     1469.   Copy of the above.
         Pp. 4.

July 18.   **1470.**   SIR NICHOLAS THROCKMORTON to CECIL.

Never saw greater confusion amongst men, for they change their opinions very often. They be always resolute to use all severity against the Queen. She is in very great danger. They will not suffer Mr. Elphinstone to have access to her. The people be greatly animated against her. — Edinburgh, 18 July 1567. *Signed.*
    Add. Endd. P. ¾.

Further pages from the *Calendar of State Papers, Foreign Elizabeth,* relating to Scotland. Directions for ordering the documents are usually available at the front of the volume.

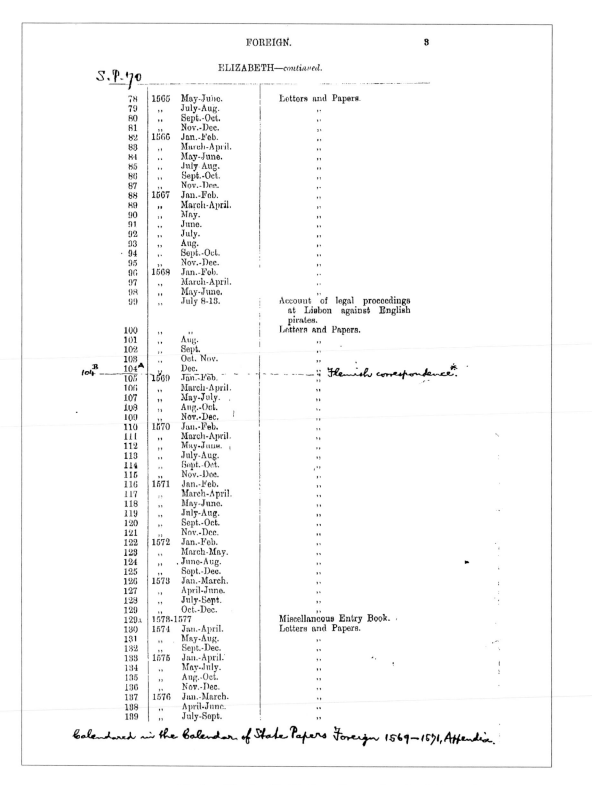

			FOREIGN.	3

ELIZABETH—*continued.*

S.P.70

78	1565	May-June.	Letters and Papers.
79	,,	July-Aug.	,,
80	,,	Sept.-Oct.	,,
81	,,	Nov.-Dec.	,,
82	1566	Jan.-Feb.	,,
83	,,	March-April.	,,
84	,,	May-June.	,,
85	,,	July Aug.	,,
86	,,	Sept.-Oct.	,,
87	,,	Nov.-Dec.	,,
88	1567	Jan.-Feb.	,,
89	,,	March-April.	,,
90	,,	May.	,,
91	,,	June.	,,
92	,,	July.	,,
93	,,	Aug.	,,
94	,,	Sept.-Oct.	,,
95	,,	Nov.-Dec.	,,
96	1568	Jan.-Feb.	,,
97	,,	March-April.	,,
98	,,	May-June.	,,
99	,,	July 8-13.	Account of legal proceedings at Lisbon against English pirates.
100	,,	,,	Letters and Papers.
101	,,	Aug.	,,
102	,,	Sept.	,,
103	,,	Oct. Nov.	,,
104ᴬ	,,	Dec.	,,
104ᴮ / 104			,, *Flemish correspondence.*
105	1569	Jan.-Feb.	,,
106	,,	March-April.	,,
107	,,	May-July.	,,
108	,,	Aug.-Oct.	,,
109	,,	Nov.-Dec.	,,
110	1570	Jan.-Feb.	,,
111	,,	March-April.	,,
112	,,	May-June.	,,
113	,,	July-Aug.	,,
114	,,	Sept.-Oct.	,,
115	,,	Nov.-Dec.	,,
116	1571	Jan.-Feb.	,,
117	,,	March-April.	,,
118	,,	May-June.	,,
119	,,	July-Aug.	,,
120	,,	Sept.-Oct.	,,
121	,,	Nov.-Dec.	,,
122	1572	Jan.-Feb.	,,
123	,,	March-May.	,,
124	,,	June-Aug.	,,
125	,,	Sept.-Dec.	,,
126	1573	Jan.-March.	,,
127	,,	April-June.	,,
128	,,	July-Sept.	,,
129	,,	Oct.-Dec.	,,
129ᴀ	1573-1577		Miscellaneous Entry Book.
130	1574	Jan.-April.	Letters and Papers.
131	,,	May-Aug.	,,
132	,,	Sept.-Dec.	,,
133	1575	Jan.-April.	,,
134	,,	May-July.	,,
135	,,	Aug.-Oct.	,,
136	,,	Nov.-Dec.	,,
137	1576	Jan.-March.	,,
138	,,	April-June.	,,
139	,,	July-Sept.	,,

Calendared in the Calendar of State Papers Foreign 1569-1571, Appendix.

The handlist for SP 70, State Papers Foreign Elizabeth, from which the calendar entries can be traced using the date.

	Reference			SP 78/304
This margin not to be used.	SP 78/304			

Folio	1777	
206	Oct 4 Nantes	Alex Keith to Stormont. He will assist the agents and always help British interests but does not think that there can be a secure channel of intelligence and must refuse Stormont's offer. Enclosed in f. 197.
208	Oct 15 Fontainebleau	Stormont to Weymouth. He has good reason to believe that the following will be discussed in the Conseil before the court leaves Fontainebleau.

    1) What France should do in the present crisis.

    2) Should she be content to give the Americans the same secret help in ships, arms and ammunition as hitherto?

    3) Or should she openly support them and engage in war with Britain?

The rebel agents press for open assistance or, if this is not possible, for the continuance of secret help with, in addition, large sums to enable them to prolong the war. They ask for 3 million sterling, which France will never grant, even if shared with Spain. He believes that Maurepas, whose opinion is decisive with the king, will not advise open war but will not declare himself against continuing to wound Britain by helping the rebels. All the other ministers would plunge into immediate war. Stormont is convinced that the government has adopted 'a fixed plan of artifice and deceit', which no representations by him can change. He will continue to make them but wishes his court to know that he is not deceived, whatever his official dispatches may imply. Most confidential.

| 210 | Oct 15 St. James' | Weymouth to Noailles. He has the admiralty's reply about ff. 54, 56, 58. The commander in chief of the navy in America has already been ordered to examine the case of the Espérance [f.58]. It is impossible to proceed further in the case of the Marthe [f. 56] without the names of the frigate or the 74 gun ship. The owners of the Elizabeth [f. 54] have permission to appeal against the court's ruling. French. |
| 213 | n.d. | Petition from the captain for the restitution of the ship Grue addressed to Maurepas. She was seized by the British at Portudal. Delivered with lord North's letter of Oct. 15. French. |

Page from a modern detailed listing of the State Papers France, **SP 78/304**

18.2 Using the Foreign Office Registers and Indexes, 1810-1890

The registers and indexes referring to general correspondence classes before 1906 can be used to find a person or subject in the bound volumes of papers without necessarily searching speculatively through a large amount of material. However, using the registers can be a complicated exercise, particularly for those interested in African, Chinese or Turkish affairs. Because of geographical and political changes the records relating to these countries are scattered through a number of Foreign Office registers and correspondence classes. It should also be noted that the registers may refer to material which has subsequently been destroyed.

You should approach these records from a geographical basis and begin by consulting the 'FO Index' which is a separate binder which can be found at the start of the main series of FO lists on the shelves in the Reference Room at Kew. It is also useful to use this index with the class descriptions in the *Current Guide* part 2. In the following example, the sample search given concerns British policy towards Russia during the 1870s after the siege of Plevna in Bulgaria. The starting point is the relevant part of the FO Index, in this case the page listing the classes in which the general registers and indexes are placed:

REGISTERS AND INDEXES OF CORRESPONDENCE

Registers of General Correspondence   FO 566

Registers (Modern Series) and Indexes of General   FO 605
    Correspondence: Microfilm Copies

Numerical (Central) Registers of General   FO 662
    Correspondence

Indexes (Printed Series) to General Correspondence   FO 409

Registers (Library Series) and Indexes of General   FO 802
    Correspondence

Indexes to General Correspondence   FO 804

Indexes to General Correspondence (Photographic Copies)

Extract from the FO index, showing registry and correspondence lettercodes

COUNTRY	CLASS NO.
RUSSIA·	
Confidential Print	FO 418, FO 490
General Correspondence	FO 65
Embassy and Consular Archives: Correspondence	FO 181
" " " " : Letter Books	FO 182
" " " " : Registers of Correspondence	FO 183
" " " " : Miscellanea	FO 184
Consulates: Archangel: Correspondence	FO 264
" : " : Letter Books	FO 265
" : " : Registers of Correspondence	FO 266
" : " : Miscellanea	FO 267
" : " : Correspondence	FO 175
" : " : (British Expedition)	
" : " : Registers of Correspondence	FO 176
" : Batum	FO 397
" : Helsingfors (Helsinki)	FO 768
(See also FINLAND: Helsinki)	
" : Leningrad (St Petersburg): Miscellanea	FO 378
" : " " " : Registers of Correspondence	FO 379
" : Libau: Correspondence	FO 396
" : " : Letter Books	FO 400
" : " : Registers of Correspondence	FO 439
" : " : Miscellanea	FO 440
" : Miscellaneous	FO 399
" : Moscow: Correspondence	FO 447
" : " : Registers of Correspondence	FO 448
" : " : Miscellanea	FO 518
" : Odessa: Correspondence	FO 257
" : " : Letter Books	FO 258
" : " : Miscellanea	FO 359
" : Riga	FO 377
" : Rostov-on-Don	FO 398
" : Tammerfors (Tampere)	FO 769
" : Vladivostock: Registers of Correspondence	FO 537
" : " : Miscellanea	FO 510

Page from the Foreign Office index, showing classes of general and embassy correspondence

The FO index shows you which record classes are available, the different types of which have been described above (see Chapter 17). In this case you should select FO 605, the microfilm copies of the fuller registers compiled by the Foreign Office Library. If you are looking for a very specific subject you may find it useful to consult the contemporary indexes which act as a form of reference to the registers.

To find the contemporary indexes covering 1810 to 1890, start by looking in the class list for FO 605 (Registers (Library Series) and Indexes of General Correspondence, Microfilm copies.) The list is arranged alphabetically by country and by date, and provides the piece (reference) number of each index and register. Not all of the registers have indexes and some are split between two microfilms.

This margin not to be used.	Reference F.O. 605	REGISTERS (MODERN SERIES) AND INDEXES OF GENERAL CORRESPONDENCE, MICROFILM COPIES		
		Date	Country	Description
	172	1857–1858	Russia	Register Vol. 9 Part 2
		1859–1860	Russia	Register Vol. 10
		1854–1859	Russia	Register Vol. 11 (Consuls)
		1861–1862	Russia	Register Vol. 12 Part 1
	173	1861–1862	Russia	Register Vol. 12 Part 2
		1863–1865	Russia	Register Vol. 13
	174	1866–1867	Russia	Register Vol. 14
		1868–1869	Russia	Register Vol. 15
		1870–1872	Russia	Register Vol. 16
	175	1873–1875	Russia	Register Vol. 17
		1876–1877	Russia	Register Vol. 18
		1878–1879	Russia	Register Vol. 19 Part 1
	176	1878–1879	Russia	Register Vol. 19 Part 2
		1880–1881	Russia	Register Vol. 20
		1882–1885	Russia	Register Vol. 21
	177	1886–1890	Russia	Register Vol. 22
		1882–1885	Russia	Register Vol. 23
		1886–1888	Russia	Register Vol. 24 Part 1
	178	1886–1888	Russia	Register Vol. 24 Part 2
		1889–1890	Russia	Register Vol. 25
		1854–1867	Russia	Register and Index. Cases
		1810–1890	Russia	Index Part 1
	179	1810–1890	Russia	Index Part 2
		1858–1881	Russia (Central Asia)	Register Vol. 1
		1882–1890	Russia (Central Asia)	Register Vol. 2
		–	Russia (Central Asia)	Index

Page from the class list of **FO 605** showing entries for Russia, late nineteenth century.

Start by noting the piece or identifying number of the index where one exists. You should then go to the Microfilm Reading Room (Romilly Room) and ask for the location of the appropriate film, giving the reference number. The microfilms are available on a self-help basis and you are allowed one at a time. The indexes are arranged alphabetically by subjects, persons, places, countries or events. In this case, the selected example refers to the Eastern Question and the capture of Plevna during the Russo-Turkish war of 1877 to 1878 (in FO 605/178).

FO 605/178 Index to Russian correspondence. In this example Russian policy in Bulgaria during the eastern crisis has been selected as follows: Plevna, battle of 19-8.23.85.91. Page 91 has been treated as an item of interest.

125

Each of the entries provides references to the relevant volume and page number of the registers, which should be noted. In this case, the entry refers to the subject, the number of the register volume (19) and indicates that material relating to Plevna can be found on pages 8, 23, 85 and 91 of that volume.

You should now consult the class list of FO 605 again, as shown in the illustration on page 124. After finding the section for Russia within the correct date range, use the references obtained from the index in conjunction with the right hand column of the list. This corresponds to the register volume number obtained from the index. When you have identified this number in the right hand column read across from it to the left hand column. This will provide the reference (piece) number for the register. In this case volume 19 is in two parts under the references FO 605/175 and FO 605/176.

Now use the reference to find the register in the appropriate microfilm of FO 605 held in the Microfilm Reading Room. In the example the correct registry entry is in FO 605/175. Use the page number obtained from the index to find the entry on the microfilm.

In the following example, page 91 has been selected.

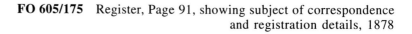

FO 605/175 Register, Page 91, showing subject of correspondence and registration details, 1878

The register, as shown on the previous page, provides some summary information about the general correspondence papers. It gives the despatch number (69), the date of despatch (16 Jan), the name of the correspondent and some details of the subject. In the extreme left or right hand margin a volume number may occasionally be found; here it is 997. This is usually the volume number in the general correspondence for the country involved, and may be identical with the PRO piece number given in the individual country class list, although this is not always the case and should not be relied upon. The details found in the register should be noted down.

Now you should consult the appropriate country class list (using the FO Index to identify it, see page 123). In this case the class for Russian general correspondence is FO 65. The format of these lists varies greatly, but it is best to approach them from the basis of the date of the despatch, the name of the sender and the description of the type of correspondence given in the list.

In this example the correspondence is most likely to be found in the papers of Lord Augustus Loftus covering January 1878 (FO 65/997).

Reference				FO 65
FO 65	Date	Description		Vol.
985	1877	Military Attaché Colonel Wellesley, Secretaries Plunkett, Scott, Doria		
986	1877	Domestic, Count Schouvaloff, M Bartholomei		
987	1877 Jan.–June	Domestic various		
988	1877 July–Dec.	" "		
989	1877 Jan.–Mar.	Proceedings in Central Asia		26
990	1877 Apr.–June	" " "		27
991	1877 July–Sept.	" " "		28
992	1877 Oct.–Dec.	" " "		29
993	1878 Jan. 1 – Feb. 15	Lord A Loftus, Drafts		
994	1878 Feb. 16 – May	" " "		
995	1878 June–Sept.	Lord A Loftus, Mr Plunkett, Drafts		
996	1878 Oct.–Dec.	" " "		
997	1878 Jan. 1–16	Lord A Loftus		
998	1878 Jan. 18 – Feb. 7	" "		
999	1878 Feb. 8–20	" "		

FO 65 Class list for General Correspondence, Russia

When the date and description have been matched up with the relevant piece number in the left hand column, order the document using the computer ordering terminals. In this case the reference for ordering is FO 65/997. When the document has been produced you should find the relevant paper in the volume by looking for the date and the despatch number, as shown in the example below.

The right-hand page reads:

Le *Messager officiel* publie dans son numéro d'hier le texte de l'adresse présentée a l'Empereur par les habitants bulgares de Plevna le 2 (14) décembre, jour ou Sa Majesté a visite cette ville:

Grand Empereur!

Les siècles de souffrances du peuple bulgare sont passés. Ils sont passés sans retour par le seul fait que Votre Majesté a jeté son epée dans le balance des destinées.

Grand Souveràin! Vous nous avez converts de votre bouclier contre la barberie des infidèles et vous nous avez donné une nouvelle vie.

Ainai que le soleil, vous avez éclairé notre pays en y venant et les chaines que nous portions depuis des siècles ont fondu comme fond a niege sous l'influence des rayons solaires.

Pouvons-nous rester indifférente à ce grand événement, des résultats duquel nous ne serons pas seuls à jouir, car nos enfants et toute notre descendance on profiterant? Par nos souffrances pendant un siége de cinq mois, nous, habitants de Plevna, nous avons compris le droit de nous mettre à la tête du peuple bulgare pour manifester à Votre Majesté ses sentiments les plus chaleureux. Nous sommes fermement persuadés que la déliverance de Plevna est l'oevre de la déliverance de l'ancienne Bulgarie; Plevna vient de ressusciter la premiere après être morte la derniere, il y a bien de siècles.

Pour graver dans le mémoire de nos descendants la date de cette résurrection et pour que l'on se rappelle dans l'avenir le bonheur que vous nous avez accordé en visitant notre ville, nous demandons à Votre Majesté l'autorisation de fonder à Plevna un gymnase de garçons et de lui donner le nom de Votre Majesté Impériale, le nom du Tsar-libérateur que chaque Bulgare ne cessera de vénérer.

La Bulgarie, comblée de vos bienfaits, Sire, vous considère comme son sauveur; elle doit vous consacrer ses enfants, qui sont l'espoir de son pays, le gage de ses progrès dans la voie de la vraie civilisation et de son union fraternelle avec la Russie.

Sous le règne d'Alexandre, fils de Georges Straschimir, l'astre de la Bulgarie s'est trouvé éteint pour de longs siècles audessus de ces mêmes hauteurs de Plevna qui l'ont vu resplendir de nouveau grâce à un autre Alexandre, couvert de l'égide de St Georges le Victorieux et justement nommé l'effroi de l'opression et le tyrannie.

Les habitants bulgares des deux sexes de la ville de Plevna, profondément et à jamais dé voués et reconnaissants.

(Suivent les signatures de l'archimandrite Constantin, de 9 ecclésiastiques et de 91 bourgeois de Plevna.)

FO 65/997 Despatch 69, Lord Augustus Loftus to earl of Derby, with copy of enclosure of *Journal de St Petersburg* transcribing an address from the inhabitants of Plevna to the Czar in December 1877, after its capture by Russian forces, dated 7-8 January 1878.

This description of how to use the registers has started with the simplest search involving indexes, registers and correspondence. There are, however, complicating factors in relation to particular types of correspondence and their arrangement. The indexes may be unreliable and should be used with caution. Despatches may be grouped under a number of headings, usually 'diplomatic', 'consular', 'consular domestic' or 'domestic' in separate parts of the registers or in separate 'cuts'. During the second half of the nineteenth century, with departmental reorganisations, other headings appeared, for example 'treaty' or 'commercial'. Slave Trade and Africa correspondence was not registered in the Library series until 1876; retrospective indexing only reached 1845. Correspondence of the Library or of departments which did not fall into any of these headings was usually put in the 'Great Britain' or 'General' registers. In approaching a search involving these headings a similar method to that described above should be used. The list for each country's general correspondence usually provides an indication of the type of correspondence in each volume, so that entries in the registers under these headings, for example consular or commercial, can be traced in them.

Another complication is the incidence of 'cases'. This term is used to describe correspondence relating to a subject which continued to be a matter of interest for a number of years and which was extracted from the general correspondence and bound separately. Usually the case volumes were kept with the general correspondence, but were occasionally removed to another correspondence class (now FO 97). The registers may not give an indication when papers may have formed part of a case, although they were usually entered at the end of the registers by country. Sometimes the word 'diary' as an entry is a clue, although these are usually very difficult to find and may be spread over a number of classes. In identifying cases it is also advisable to consult a manuscript register of cases to 1905 which is available on open access in the Reference Room at Kew. This is arranged by countries and also has an index to subjects, persons and vessels. If a subject may have been of importance to governments in the nineteenth century it is worth checking this index before proceeding to the general correspondence and its registers, as it is marked up with the current references of the case volumes.

18.3 Using the Foreign Office Registers and Indexes, 1891-1905

As a result of registry reforms in the Foreign Office in 1891, the Library series of indexes was discontinued. This means that for searches after this date the departmental diaries, or registers, created in the Foreign Office departments throughout the nineteenth century must be used instead. These registers are in the class FO 566. During the period 1891 to 1905 the separate departmental registers created for diplomatic, consular, commercial and treaty correspondence were continued with a new system of standard signs and abbreviations. These registers also have indexes, copies of some of which are now arranged into a separate class, FO 738 Indexes to General Correspondence, photographic copies 1891-1905. These indexes refer mainly to diplomatic correspondence and may be used to trace individual items, but they are by no means reliable and should be treated with caution. It is also possible to browse through the registers themselves rather than relying on the indexes.

The indexes should be approached in the same way as described above. Taking another example, this time the Triple Alliance of Germany, Austria and Italy formed in 1894 and possible adherence to it by other central European states, the diplomatic indexes can be used to trace reports received by the Foreign Office on the countries involved. In this case, the register for Roumania has been selected as an example.

Use the class list of FO 738 to find the reference number of the index, looking for the appropriate area. In this case the reference is FO 738/31.

This margin not to be used.	Reference P.O. 738	GENERAL CORRESPONDENCE: INDEXES TO GENERAL CORRESPONDENCE	
		Date	Description
	'21	1891–1905	Hayti
	22	1891–1905	Italy
	23	1891–1906	Japan
	24	1891–1905	Mexico
	25	1891–1905	Montenegro
	26	1891–1905	Morocco
	27	1891–1905	Netherlands
	28	1891–1905	Newfoundland
			Norway see Sweden and Norway
	29	1891–1905	Pacific Islands
	30	1891–1905	Portugal
	31	1891–1905	Roumania
	32	1891–1905	Russia

Page from the class list for **FO 738**, with highlighted entry showing the index for Roumania.

When you have identified the references go to the indexes, most of which are available on open access in the Reference Room at Kew. Material within them is arranged alphabetically by the first two letters of the subject or person. Once you have identified an item of interest, note the page number and the year of the register for the entry concerned. In this example the entry describing a report of Roumanian adherence to the treaty has been used.

Subjects		Persons	
	Register year page		Register year page
Triple Alliance rumoured adhesion of Roumania	1897 7		

Diagram of manuscript index, **FO 738/31**, Roumania.

Note down the year and page number given in the registry columns.

Now go to the class list for the Registers of General Correspondence, 1817-1920, in FO 566. Use it to identify the appropriate register, using the country and date as a guide. Note down the reference number for the register needed. For this example the appropriate reference is FO 566/911, which is the only volume which corresponds to the date range and subject matter.

910	1887-1892	Roumania (Balkan Commercial States)	O.
911	1890-1900	**Roumania; Diplomatic Serbia**	**G.H.**
-	1893-1898	Roumania Commercial (Balkan States)	see Balkan States (O.)
912	1896-1905	Roumania; Serbia Consular	M.
913	1899-1905	Roumania Commercial (Balkan States)+	Winting
914	1901-1905	Roumania; Serbia	Diplomatic	G.H.

Page of the class list for **FO 566**, with highlighted entry for Roumania.

Many of these registers (the diplomatic ones) are available on shelves in the Reference Room, although not all. When the register is located, the correct entry can be found using the page number noted from the index. Look first for the year, which may be labelled or in a 'cut'. Once you have found the year, look for the page number in that section (in this case, 7). As the index entry suggests that the report is an incoming one, look at the left hand page of the register for the matching description. The registers are set out in the manner shown in the illustration below.

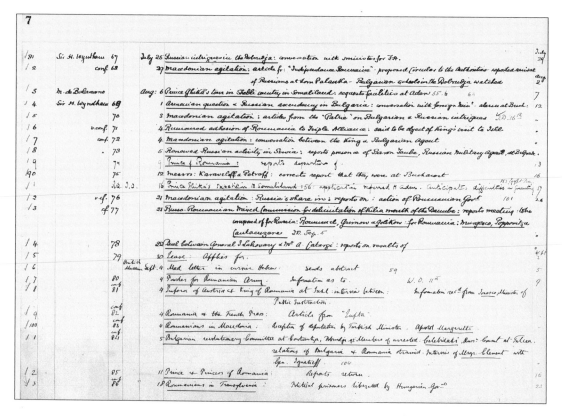

FO 566/911   Page 7 of register covering Roumanian diplomatic correspondence

The left hand page refers to incoming despatches, and includes, by column: the registry number; the name of the correspondent; the despatch number; the date of the despatch; the subject; any cross reference to other registry numbers, and the date of reply. If there are further numbers at the end of the description this means that there are related papers, which can be traced in the same register. If they are in black they refer to incoming correspondence and can be traced on the left hand pages. If they are in red they refer to the outgoing correspondence which is registered on the right hand pages.

To find the actual correspondence noted in the registers you will need to note the name of the correspondent and the despatch number given in the entry. You should then use the class list for the general correspondence for the country in question. The class number can be identfied from the FO Index as mentioned above; in this case it is FO 104. Although the format of the lists may vary, on the whole the correspondence is arranged in chronological order and divided into subject headings. In this search the appropriate entry is that marked 'diplomatic' on the right hand side of the list and the correct reference is FO 104/119. Once the piece number has been identified the document can be ordered using the computer terminals.

Use the despatch number (in this case no. 71) and date to trace the correspondence once the volume has been produced.

```
                    GENERAL CORRESPONDENCE.    ROUMANIA

   Reference      Date                        Description

   F.O.104

      112        1894           Sir J. Walsham,         Diplomatic.
                                Sir H. Wyndham.         Despatches.

      113        1894           Mr. Townley.            Diplomatic
                                                        Telegrams and
                                                        Paraphrases.

      114        1894           Sir J. Walsham,         Consular
                                Sir H. Wyndham,         Commercial
                                Mr. Townley.            Treaty
                                                        Africa.

      115        1894           Consuls General        Diplomatic
                                at Galatz.              Consular
                                Sanderson, Trotter,     Commercial
                                Crawford.               Treaty.
                                Vice-Consuls at Braila,
                                Bucharest, Sulina.
                                Churchward, Browne,
                                Liddell, Vecqueray
                                Domestic.
                                M. Belaceano,
                                M. Nedeyano.

      116        1894           Various,                Diplomatic
                                                        Consular
                                                        Commercial
                                                        Treaty.

      117        1892-1894      Extradition Treaty.

      118        1891-1894      Commercial Treaty.

      119        1895           Sir H. Wyndham,         Diplomatic.
                                Col. Trotter.           Correspondence
                                                        and Telegrams.

      120        1895           do.                     Consular
                                do.                     Treaty
                                                        Africa.

      121        1895           do.                     Commercial.
                                do.

      122        1895           Consuls General         Diplomatic
                                at Galatz.              Consular
                                Trotter, Crawford,      Commercial
                                Bennett.                Treaty.
                                Vice-Consuls at
                                Braila, Galatz.
                                Churchward, Bennett.
                                Domestic.
                                M. Balaceano,
                                M. Nedeyano.
```

Copy of list of **FO 104**

242

Sinaia
August 4. 1895.

No 71
Very Confidential

My Lord,

Rumours have been current here that the chief object of the visit of Their Majesties The King and Queen of Roumania to The Emperor of Austria is formally to join the Triple Alliance in consequence of recent events in Bulgaria, while there are also rumours current that that step was taken about eighteen months ago.

The visit to the Austrian Court was, I am informed by my Austrian colleague, arranged last spring, King Charles not having seen the Emperor for some time, and was not immediately due to recent events in Bulgaria.

Whether Roumania has formally bound herself to the Triple Alliance by a written engagement or not, I cannot say, but His Majesty The King informed me privately and Confidentially

The Marquess of Salisbury, KG
etc   etc

FO 104/119 No 71 Sir H Wyndham, Sinaia, to Marquess of Salisbury, Aug 4 1895.

confidentially last December that his foreign policy was entirely in accord with that of the Powers who formed the Triple Alliance.

I have the honour to be, with the highest respect, my Lord, Your Lordship's most obedient, humble servant

Hugh M. Wyndham.

FO 104/119   No 71 Sir H Wyndham, Sinaia, to Marquess of Salisbury, Aug 4 1895.

To identify material in the consular, commercial and and treaty papers of the Foreign Office, the process is essentially the same, except that the original indexes must be consulted. There are separate indexes for the different categories of correspondence. You should start by using the class list for FO 804, which contains Indexes to General Correspondence, 1891 to 1905. Pieces FO 804/51-59 are especially relevant as they are the separate Consular, Treaty and Commercial departmental indexes. These documents have to be ordered by using the computer ordering system. The indexes are similar in format to the diplomatic registers in FO 738, although some of them use country code letters which should be noted. (These were assigned by the departments and there was no uniform list of codes between them). A full list of the country codes can be found in appendix IIc of *The Records of the Foreign Office*. As explained above, these indexes refer to the registers in FO 566. After using the indexes you should look in the list of FO 566 for the appropriate register. The right hand column of the list will give you the code and series (commercial, consular, etc) which you can match up from the information provided in the indexes.

18.4 Using the Foreign Office Registers, 1906-1951

18.4.1 Registers and indexes 1906-1919

From 1906 the general correspondence of the Foreign Office is arranged in a series of broad subject classes, for example political, treaty, or consular, and is no longer divided into individual country classes. After 1920 these classes are divided by department and then subdivided alphabetically by countries and/or subjects.

The Foreign Office produced a centralised index which refers to these records. It is arranged by year and then alphabetically by subjects, persons and places. For the correspondence between 1906 and 1919 the PRO has the original Foreign Office card index, which is now available on open access in the Reference Room at Kew.

For the period 1906 to 1919 the card index is particularly useful for locating specific material relating to individuals or to subjects or countries. It does not, however, have sufficient information for documents to be ordered immediately from it. You may need to go through other record classes before obtaining a document ordering reference for the record which you seek. Before 1910, this process involves using Foreign Office registers of correspondence as well as class lists. After 1910 it is more common to go straight to the class list after interpreting the entries on the index card.

Using the Index for pre-1910 material:

As an example, supposing that you were interested in investigating Anglo-German relations before 1914, you might select the following entry in the card index under the heading 'Great Britain: Royal Family and Court' for further investigation.

Great Britain			Royal Family and Court
18	3382	06	Letter from the king to the German Emperor The emp's hopes that all differences between himself and the king might be removed and friendly rel's established

Foreign Office index card for 1906

136

The index card shown as an example provides you with the following information:

The first line is for the general subject heading.

The first column on the left contains the country or subject number (here it is 18).

The second column includes the number of the Foreign Office paper to which the index card refers.

The third column is used for the year. This is usually abbreviated, as in this case, where '06' means 1906. The last column provides a description of the contents of the document.

There are a number of steps to go through before you can order your document. The Foreign Office index cards do not carry any current PRO references and you will need to identify them from the registers and lists in the Reference Room.

Your first step is to find out which country or subject the card refers to. You can get this information from the number in the first column of the card and by using the key located on top of the index cabinet. Each range of numbers, or numbers with a letter, refers to a particular record country or subject. In this case '18' is the index number for Germany. Each number also comes within the indexing system of a particular class of records. You can also trace which class is referred to by using the reference board. In this case the paper is in the general correspondence in FO 371. But you will not be able to identify the correct reference from this list unless you have a <u>file number</u> as well as a paper number.

The next step is to find out which file contains the paper sought. Each department, as explained above, arranged its papers in files by this time, and both papers and files were given identifying numbers. To find this out you will need to look at the registers of Foreign Office correspondence in FO 566.

Find the class list for FO 566 and look for the date, the country and the country heading (18) on the right hand side of the list. In this case the right entry is the 1906 diplomatic register for Germany. Read across to the left hand column and note the number given. This is the document piece reference. In this case the full reference is FO 566/765.

758	1896–1900	" †	Diplomatic	N.
759	1896–1900	Germany (Consulates)†	Consular	F.
760	1896–1905	Germany	Treaty	G.
761	1899–1905	" ‡	Commercial	Wanting
762	1899–1905	Germany (Coburg and Darmstadt)	Diplomatic	P.Q.
763	1901–1905	Germany†	"	N.
764	1901–1905	" †	Consular	F.
765	1906–1907	"	Diplomatic	18

*.First Hague Peace Conference.
† Except Coburg and Darmstadt.
‡ For 1903 and 1905 see France; & FO 566/1663,1666,1669,1670, 167?

Copy of **FO 566** list, with FO 566/765 highlighted.

Some diplomatic registers are available in the Reference Room and do not need to be ordered by the computer. These are usually marked 'Reference Room' in the list and are available for most of the pre-1910 material.

Once you have found the register, look for the appropriate date which may be in its own cut. Then look for the registry number (in this case 3382, as given on the index card) in the left hand column of the left hand pages which refer to incoming correspondence. In this example the correct registry page is as follows:

FO 566/765 Page of register, showing incoming correspondence.

The register can give you a good deal of information about the document, for example whether it was printed, who sent it, date of receipt, the last paper referring to the same subject, and a summary of contents. The most important information to note is that in the 'kept with' column. This is the number of the file in which the paper was kept. In this example the file number is 30.

The last column, headed 'forward reference', can also be used to trace associated correspondence. The number 3451G refers to a further entry in the registry. When this is written in black, it usually refers to the incoming correspondence registered on the left hand side of the page. When it is written in red it usually refers to the outgoing correspondence which is entered on the right hand pages of the register. In this case the number is in black, so it refers to other incoming reports. The G refers to the code for Munich, which can be found under another 'cut' in the register. (Not all registers are arranged in this manner but there are usually internal clues as to how the forward referencing system works). The relevant page of the register in this example is as follows:

FO 566/765   Forward page of register

This entry refers to more associated papers, under the forward reference 3526D. To find this entry in the register the same procedure should be followed.

Once you have the file number, go to the list for FO 371. (The board on the index cabinet will have given you the relevant class for the paper sought). Look for the date first (1906), then the country (Germany). Look in the right hand column of the list for the file number (30). When you have found the file number read across to the left hand column. This gives you the piece reference needed to order the document on the computer. In this example the full document ordering reference is FO 371/75.

```
                    GENERAL CORRESPONDENCE

                         POLITICAL

Reference     Date              Description

F.O  371

   63         1906    Egypt.        File 1880
                                        (pp.17205 - 26692) 1 vol.

  ´64         1906    do.           do. 1880
  C                                     (pp.26695 - 43490) 1 vol.

  | 65        1906    do.           Files  9267 - 20270   1 vol.

  ´66         1906    do.   File 20302 (Denishawi Incident) 1 vo.

  , 67        1906    do.           Files  20305 - 29989   1 vol.

  ( 68        1906    do.           do.   30356 - 43854   1 vol.

    69        1906    France.       do.      17 -    704   1 vol.

    70        1906    do.           do.     705 -   2192   1 vol.

    71        1906    do.           do.    2328 -   8034   1 vol.

  | 72        1906    do.           do.    8733 -  22002   1 vol.

    73        1906    do.           do.   22063 -  31434   1 vol.

    74        1906    do.           do.   31553 -  43374   1 vol.

  -           1906    General. See
                      F.O. 371/165 -
                      168

  | 75        1906    Germany.      do.      30 -   1575   1 vol.

    76        1906    do.           do.    1638 -   5404   1 vol.

    77        1906    do.           do.    5910 -  15932   1 vol.

    78        1906    do.           do.   16143 -  27085   1 vol.

    79        1906    do.           do.   27664 -  37099   1 vol.

    80        1906    do.           do.   37156 -  43837   1 vol.

    81        1906    Greece.
                1906  Hayti and San
                      Domingo.                             1 vol.

    82        1906    Italy.        do.     431 -  20554   1 vol.

    83        1906    do.           do.   20555 -  42800   1 vol.

  X 84        1906    Japan.        do.     253 -   1434   1 vol.

  X 85        1906    do.           do.    1548 -  10776   1 vol.

  ✓86         1906    do.           do.   10994 -  22961   1 vol.
```

FO 371   Copy of class list, covering Germany, 1906.

When your document had been delivered you will need to locate the papers in what may be a very large bound volume of correspondence. Use the paper number (in this example 3382) to find the right paper.

It is useful to note when using these index cards that all country or subject numbers falling between 1 and 59 refer to material which can be found amongst the records of the political departments (in the class FO 371). If the country or subject number is above 100, the paper is probably in the correspondence of another department. The explanatory board will tell you which one is referred to.

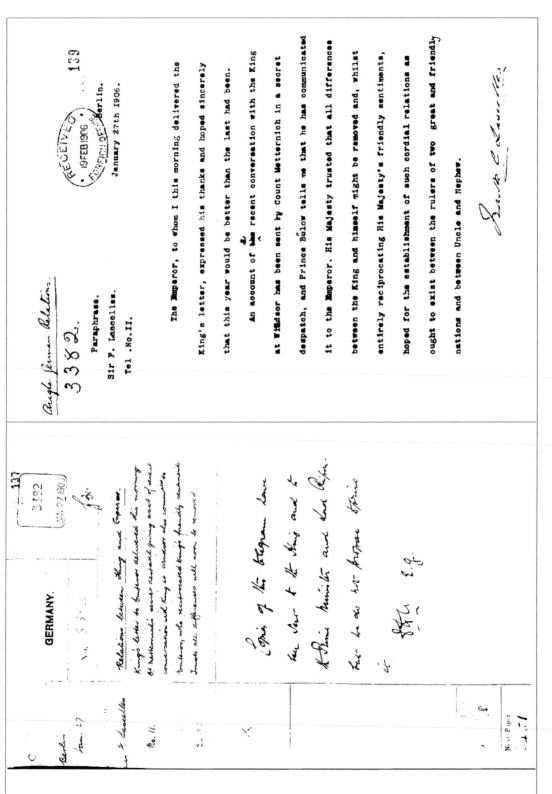

The Emperor, to whom I this morning delivered the

King's letter, expressed his thanks and hoped sincerely

that this year would be better than the last had been.

An account of the recent conversation with the King

at Windsor has been sent by Count Metternich in a secret

despatch, and Prince Bülow tells me that he has communicated

it to the Emperor. His Majesty trusted that all differences

between the King and himself might be removed and, whilst

entirely reciprocating His Majesty's friendly sentiments,

hoped for the establishment of such cordial relations as

ought to exist between the rulers of two great and friendly

nations and between Uncle and Nephew.

Paraphrase.

Sir F. Lascelles.

Tel.No.II.

3382.

Anglo German Relations.

RECEIVED
19 FEB 1906
FOREIGN OFFICE Berlin.
January 27th 1906.

139

GERMANY.

FO 371/75, paper 3382   Copy of file cover and first page of correspondence

142

There are other complications. The number may be prefixed by a letter. For example 'N' before the number means that the paper is part of the correspondence of the News Department (FO 395) and 'W' means that the paper is in the war series for the country concerned. (The war prefix only occurs for papers dated 1914 to 1919). The card index does not refer to the papers of the Library (FO 370), the Chief Clerk's Department (FO 366) or the Foreign Trade Department (FO 833). It should also be borne in mind that the index is a contemporary system and contains many references to papers that have subsequently been weeded and destroyed.

Using the Index after 1910:

For much of the period 1906 to 1909 the index cards only provide the paper number (as above). After 1909 the cards usually contain the file number as well. This is expressed in a number of ways. The number may be marked with an 'F' as in the example below, or simply 'file'. The number may be underlined to show that it refers to the file, or expressed as a type of fraction, for example, $\frac{26616}{91}$

The file number is on the base of the entry and the paper number on top. It is also worth noting that where there are two numbers usually the lower (numerically speaking) number is the file number and the higher the paper number.

Where the paper and file numbers are the same this can be an indication that the entire file is of relevance to the subject noted on the index card. In general, the file takes its number from the first paper on it. The examples below illustrate how the file numbers can be expressed:

This card tells you that all the papers can be found in file 7014 of the general correspondence of the political departments in 1912.

Great Britain			Foreign Relations
50	f 7014	12	Attitude to be adopted towards Belgium, etc

Example from the card index: Great Britain Foreign Relations,
attitude to be adopted towards Belgium, 1912

```
                    GENERAL CORRESPONDENCE
                         POLITICAL

   Reference      Date              Description

   F.O. 371

     1551         1912      Venezuela.    Files    684 -    4320    1 vol.

     1552         1912         do.        do.      4595 - 54,875    1 vol.

     1553         1912      Miscellaneous do.        23 -     382    1 vol.
                            (General).

     1554         1912         do.        do.       420 -     646    1 vol.

     1555         1912         do.        do.       856 -    3272    1 vol.

     1556         1912         do.        do.      3407 -    6398    1 vol.

     1557         1912         do.        do.      6485 - 13,337    1 vol.

     1558         1912         do.        do.    12,343 - 16,031
                                                    (papers
                                                  16,031 - 18,071)
                                                                    1 vol.

     1559         1912         do.        do.    16,031 (papers
                                                  18,122 - 30,749) -
                                                            17,558
                                                                    1 vol.

     1560         1912         do.        do.    17,774 - 23,803    1 vol.

     1561         1912         do.        do.    23,901 - 35,805    1 vol.

     1562         1912         do.        do.    35,726 - 55,702    1 vol.

     1563         1912      America       do.        81 -    1002    1 vol.
                            (General).

     1564         1912         do.        do.      5388 - 16,958    1 vol.

     1565         1912         do.        do.    17,283 - 55,687    1 vol.

     1566         1912      Case 607.   Newfoundland Fisheries      1 vol.

     1567         1912      Case 608.   New Hebridean Affairs
                                           (papers    18 - 17,249)  1 vol.

     1568         1912         do.        (do..  17,254 - 38,676)   1 vol.

     1569         1912         do.        (do.   39,098 - 55,819)   1 vol.

     1570         1913      Abyssinia.   Files    423 -    7252     1 vol.

     1571         1913         do.        do.      7267 -   23762    1 vol.

     1572         1913         do.        do.     24160 -   57638    1 vol.

     1573         1913      Argentine.    do.       627 -   25225    1 vol.

     1574         1913         do.        do.      26222 -  58154    1 vol.
```

FO 371   Sample page of list

As you already have the file number you do not need to search through the registers in FO 566. Instead you should go straight to the relevant class list, using the information given on the explanatory boards, which in this case is FO 371. In this example, look for the year 1912, the heading miscellaneous (General) and the file number. Read across to the left hand column. This gives you the piece reference needed to order the correspondence on the computer; in this example the full reference is FO 371/1557. When the document arrives, look for the appropriate date and paper number in the volume in the same way as outlined above.

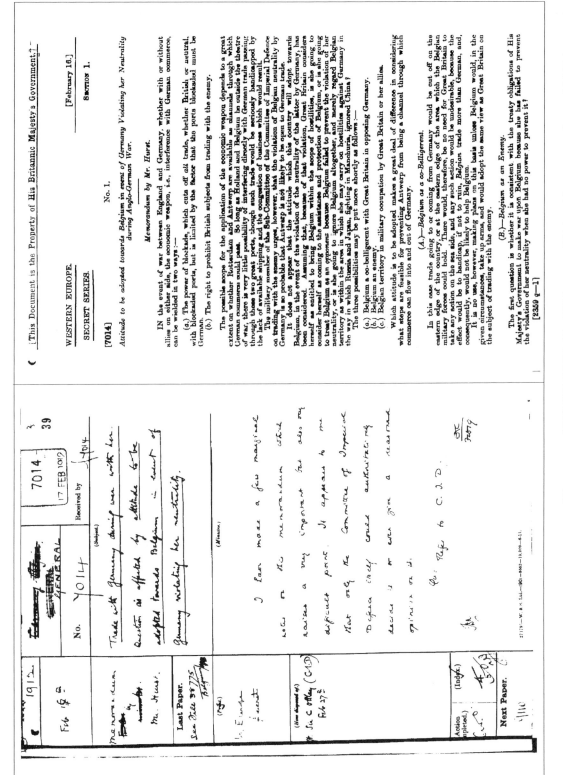

[This Document is the Property of His Britannic Majesty's Government.]

WESTERN EUROPE. [February 16.]

SECRET SERIES. SECTION 1.

[7014] No. 1.

Attitude to be adopted towards Belgium in event of Germany violating her Neutrality during Anglo-German War.

Memorandum by Mr. Hurst.

IN the event of war between England and Germany, whether with or without allies on either side, the economic weapon, i.e., interference with German commerce, can be wielded in two ways:—

(a.) The power of blockade, which cuts off *all* trade, whether British or neutral, with blockaded ports, but is limited by the factor that the ports blockaded must be German.

(b.) The right to prohibit British subjects from trading with the enemy.

The possible scope for the application of the economic weapon depends to a great extent on whether Rotterdam and Antwerp are available as channels through which German commerce could pass. So long as Holland and Belgium lie outside the theatre of war, there is very little possibility of interfering directly with German trade passing through these two great ports, though such trade would be seriously handicapped by the lack of available shipping and the congestion of business which would result.

The military member of the Sub-Committee of the Committee of Imperial Defence on trading with the enemy urges, however, that the violation of Belgian neutrality by Germany is improbable that Antwerp is not likely to be open to German trade.

It does not appear that the attitude which this country will adopt towards Belgium, in the event of the violation of the neutrality of the latter by Germany, has been considered. Assuming that, because of that violation, Great Britain considers herself as entitled to bring Belgium within the scope of hostilities, is she going to consider herself as coming to the assistance and protection of Belgium, or is she going to treat Belgium as an *opponent* because Belgium failed to prevent the violation of her neutrality, or is she going to ignore Belgium altogether, and merely regard Belgian territory as within the area in which she may carry on hostilities against Germany in the way in which Russia and Japan, fighting in Manchuria, ignored China? The three possibilities may be put more shortly as follows:—

(a.) Belgium a co-belligerent with Great Britain in opposing Germany.

(b.) Belgium an enemy.

(c.) Belgian territory in military occupation by Great Britain or her allies.

Which attitude is to be adopted makes a great deal of difference in considering what steps are feasible for preventing Antwerp from being a channel through which commerce can flow into and out of Germany.

(A.)—Belgium as a co-Belligerent.

In this case trade going to or coming from Germany would be cut off on the eastern edge of the country, or at the eastern edge of the area which the Belgian military forces could hold. There would, therefore, be no need for Great Britain to take any action on the sea side, and any such action would be undesirable, because the effect would be to handicap, if not to ruin, *Belgian* trade more than German, and, consequently, would not be likely to help Belgium.

It is no use, however, making plans on this basis unless Belgium would, in the given circumstances, take up arms, and would adopt the same view as Great Britain on the subject of trading with the enemy.

(B.)—Belgium as an Enemy.

The first question is whether it is consistent with the treaty obligations of His Majesty's Government to make war upon Belgium because she has failed to prevent the violation of her neutrality when she had no power to prevent it?

[2359 g—1]

File cover of **FO 371/1557**, file 7014, paper 7014, with memorandum of 16 February by Hurst on British attitudes to a possible German violation of Belgian neutrality

Great Britain			Foreign Relations Russia
38	26616/91	19	PM's statement of policy regarding Br. intervention in Russia

Index card: Great Britain Foreign Relations Russia: Prime Minister's statement of policy regarding British intervention in Russia.

Most index cards after 1910 show the file number as in the above example.

The paper number here is 26616 and the file number is 91. You should follow the same steps as outlined in the above examples to find the correct ordering reference.

18.4.2 Registers and Indexes, 1920-1951

For the period 1920 to 1951, the indexes are available in printed form in the Reference Room at Kew. There are usually four volumes to a year, which have a similar content to the pre-1920 indexes. They are arranged alphabetically and include references to persons, countries, ships, companies, places and subjects.

Each individual reference in the index consists of a short description and an identifying code, as shown in the example page below, relating to the Munich crisis:

469

Chamberlain, Neville, Rt. Hon. (continued).
Telegraphic appeal from President of Ecuador not to spare any effort to reach peaceful solution of Sudeten German problem. C11256/1941/18.
Visit to Godesberg: report to French Ministers on conversation with Herr Hitler, 22nd-23rd September. C11264/1941/18.
Message of appreciation to M. Daladier for his loyal and helpful co-operation during negotiations with Herr Hitler regarding Sudeten German problem: publication. C11355/C11356/13/17.
Desire of people of Province of Zealand to offer a present in admiration and gratitude of his work in interest of peace: suggestion that monies collected should be devoted to local charity in his name. C11438/C11722/C11805/10318/29.
— Further similar case. C13035/11591/4.
Conversations with Herr Hitler at Munich following Czechoslovak settlement, C11532/42/18.
Interview with Völkischer Beobachter at Munich. C11535/42/18.
Munich conference: speech following: reaction in Italy. R7973/23/22.
Economic situation in South-East Europe: conversation with Herr Hitler.

Chamberlain, Neville, Rt. Hon. (continued).
Congratulatory telegram from Egyptian Prime Minister on success in averting war: reply. J3769/3537/16.
Congratulatory messages from Egypt following European crisis. J3894/3537/16.
Congratulatory telegram from Sardar Bahadur Nawab Mehrab Khan on peace efforts of. N5370/5370/97 (file).
Message to Herr Hitler prior to latter's speech in Berlin on 5th October. C11878/1041/18.
Conversation with Herr Hitler after Munich Conference and signature of "no more war" document: report on: Cabinet paper. C11970/11169/18.
— With Signor Mussolini: report. C11970/11169/18.
Czechoslovak crisis: messages exchanged with President Roosevelt. C12083/1941/18.
Message of congratulation for his intervention with Herr Hitler while in Germany, from King Boris: message of thanks returned to King Boris. C12172/C14537/5302/18.
Peace efforts during Czechoslovak crisis: gold medal presented by Committee "France-Italie" of Toulouse. C12369/11596/17.
Presentation of musical work by wife of General Laborde. C13650/11596/17.
British commitments to France in event of

Foreign Office index, p. 469, showing entries for 1938, Neville Chamberlain: Conversations with Herr Hitler after the Munich Conference and signature of 'no more war' document: report on: cabinet paper: C11970/11169/18 with Signor Mussolini, report C11970/11169/18

If you were studying the Munich agreement, the entry marked in the diagram might well be a document which you would need to examine. In order to do so, you would need to find out the current PRO ordering reference for the document, as the reference you are given here is the original Foreign Office file and paper number and not the modern PRO reference.

The references given in the index are made up of the following parts:

> The letter at the beginning of the code refers to the Foreign Office department within which the paper was used, and is followed by the paper number or numbers.

> The second number is the file to which the paper belongs.

> The final number refers to a subject or country category.

The meanings of the departmental codes and the country and subject numbers can be found by referring to the key tables at the front of each volume of the index. You will need to note all these references to find the correct class list and reference for ordering the document. Part of the key is shown below:

(iv)

15. The following is a list of the index-numbers and departmental designations used in this index :—

Abyssinia (*see* Ethiopia)...	1	Germany	18	Serb-Croat-Slovene King-	
Afghanistan (*see* Central Asia)		Greece	19	dom (*see* Yugoslavia).	
Africa: General	(60)	Guatemala (*see* Central		Siam...	40
Albania	(90)	America).		Slavery and Native Labour	(52)
America: General ...	(51)	Hayti and Santo Domingo	20	Southern: General	(67)
Arabia	(91)	Health (*see* supplemen-		Soviet Union	(38)
Argentina	2	tary numbers).		Spain	41
Arms Traffic	(95)	Hejaz and Nejd (*see* Saudi		Sudan (*see* Egypt and Sudan).	
Austria	3	Arabia).		Sweden	42
Aviation (*see* Commercial		Honduras (*see* Central		Switzerland	43
Aviation).		America).		Syria	(89)
Baltic States	(59)	Hungary	21	Thailand (*see* Siam).	
Belgium and Luxemburg...	4	International Rivers (*see*		Transjordan (*see* Palestine	
Bolivia	5	supplementary numbers).		and Transjordan).	
Brazil	6	Iran (*see* Persia).		Turkey	44
Bulgaria	7	Iraq	(93)	United States	45
Cables and Wireless (*see*		Italy ...	22	Uruguay	46
supplementary numbers).		Japan	23	Vatican	(57)
Censorship (*see* supple-		Jugo-Slavia (*see* Yugoslavia).		Venezuela	47
mentary numbers).		Latvia (*see* Baltic States).		Refugees	48
Central America ...	8	League of Nations...	(98)	Co-ordination	49
Central Asia	(97)	Liberia	24	Yugoslavia ...	(92)
Central: General	(62)	Lithuania (*see* Baltic States).		General: Miscellaneous ...	50
Chile...	9	Luxemburg (*see* Belgium		America: General...	51
China	10	und Luxemburg).		Slavery and Native Labour	52
Colombia	11	Saudi Arabia	25	Economic	53
Commercial Aviation (*see*		Mexico	26	Ecuador	54
supplementary numbers).		Morocco	28	Poland	55
Communications and		Nejd (*see* Saudi Arabia).		Finland	56
Transit	(18)	Netherlands	29	Vatican	57
Contract Labour (*see*		Nicaragua (*see* Central America).		Baltic States	59
Slavery and Native		Northern: General	(62)	Africa: General	60

Sample page from printed indexes to correspondence, showing country codes. The key also provides subject and departmental codes.

Using the key the reference can be de-coded. The prefix C refers to the Central Department, the paper number is 11970 and the file number is 11169. The final index number (18) tells you that the country referred to is Germany. Sometimes there may be more than one paper number in the reference, for example as in the reference C12126/C12156/39/36. This means that papers 12126 and 12156 of the Central Department (C) are both held on file 39 of the political correspondence for Portugal (36).

To find the right class list you should use the information given in the information boards provided near the indexes. In the Munich example the document forms part of the correspondence of the political departments (FO 371). The FO 371 class lists are arranged by year, then by department, and then alphabetically by country. In this example look in the class list of FO 371 for 1938, then for the Central Department and then the country (Germany). To identify the correct piece number a search should be made down the right hand side of the page which includes file numbers. When the file number, or the range within which it lies, has been located, trace across to the left hand column. This will give you the reference (piece) number needed to order the original. Some files are split, and ranges of paper numbers appear in the right hand column. You should select the range containing the relevant paper number and then look at the left hand column for the reference. In this case the correct reference for requisitioning the document is FO 371/21785.

If the file number sought does not appear in the list, the file has not been selected for permanent preservation.

This margin not to be used.	Reference	Date	Description	Files
	F.O.371		Germany – contd.	
	21784	1938	Sudeten and Czechoslovak affairs: Munich and after	11169 (pp.11669–11886)
	21785	1938	" " " " "	11169 (pp.11887–12144)
	21786	1938	" " " " "	11169 (pp.12164–12420)
	21787	1938	" " " " "	11169 (pp.12421–13305)
	21788	1938	" " " " "	11169 (pp.13306–14363)

Page of list of **FO 371** covering 1938

When you receive your document you will need to look through the volume to find the file bearing the reference given in the index, in this case C11970/11169/18. The diagram below shows where this will appear on the file cover.

The file cover provides other information, for example the file numbers of next and previous papers, and the comments of officials who may have seen and commented on the paper. Usually a circulation list is given, as is the case in this example. If the paper or papers required do not appear in the file it is also possible that the paper has not been selected for permanent preservation. In this case it may be worth while checking the Confidential Print to see if it has been included there.

FO 371/21785   C11970/11169/18, file cover of account of conversations, dated October 1938

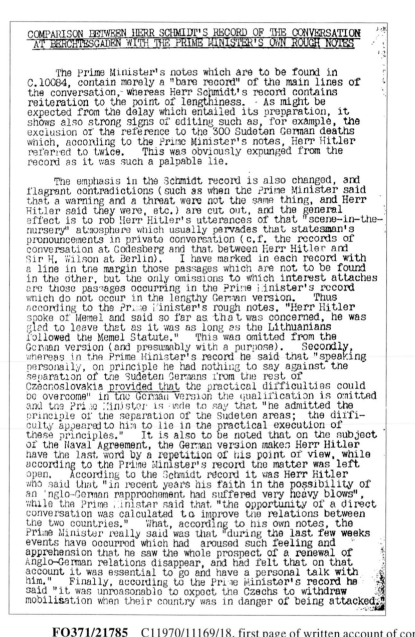

COMPARISON BETWEEN HERR SCHMIDT'S RECORD OF THE CONVERSATION
AT BERCHTESGADEN WITH THE PRIME MINISTER'S OWN ROUGH NOTES

The Prime Minister's notes which are to be found in
C.10084, contain merely a "bare record" of the main lines of
the conversation, whereas Herr Schmidt's record contains
reiteration to the point of lengthiness. As might be
expected from the delay which entailed its preparation, it
shows also strong signs of editing such as, for example, the
exclusion of the reference to the 300 Sudeten German deaths
which, according to the Prime Minister's notes, Herr Hitler
referred to twice. This was obviously expunged from the
record as it was such a palpable lie.

The emphasis in the Schmidt record is also changed, and
flagrant contradictions (such as when the Prime Minister said
that a warning and a threat were not the same thing, and Herr
Hitler said they were, etc.) are cut out, and the general
effect is to rob Herr Hitler's utterances of that "scene-in-the-
nursery" atmosphere which usually pervades that statesman's
pronouncements in private conversation (c.f. the records of
conversation at Godesberg and that between Herr Hitler and
Sir H. Wilson at Berlin). I have marked in each record with
a line in the margin those passages which are not to be found
in the other, but the only omissions to which interest attaches
are those passages occurring in the Prime Minister's record
which do not occur in the lengthy German version. Thus
according to the Prime Minister's rough notes, "Herr Hitler
spoke of Memel and said so far as that was concerned, he was
glad to leave that as it was as long as the Lithuanians
followed the Memel Statute." This was omitted from the
German version (and presumably with a purpose). Secondly,
whereas in the Prime Minister's record he said that "speaking
personally, on principle he had nothing to say against the
separation of the Sudeten Germans from the rest of
Czechoslovakia provided that the practical difficulties could
be overcome" in the German version the qualification is omitted
and the Prime Minister is made to say that "he admitted the
principle of the separation of the Sudeten areas; the diffi-
culty appeared to him to lie in the practical execution of
these principles." It is also to be noted that on the subject
of the Naval Agreement, the German version makes Herr Hitler
have the last word by a repetition of his point of view, while
according to the Prime Minister's record the matter was left
open. According to the Schmidt record it was Herr Hitler
who said that "in recent years his faith in the possibility of
an 'nglo-German rapprochement had suffered very heavy blows",
while the Prime Minister said that "the opportunity of a direct
conversation was calculated to improve the relations between
the two countries." What, according to his own notes, the
Prime Minister really said was that "during the last few weeks
events have occurred which had aroused such feeling and
apprehension that he saw the whole prospect of a renewal of
Anglo-German relations disappear, and had felt that on that
account it was essential to go and have a personal talk with
him." Finally, according to the Prime Minister's record he
said "it was unreasonable to expect the Czechs to withdraw
mobilisation when their country was in danger of being attacked."

FO371/21785 C11970/11169/18, first page of written account of conversations,
dated October 1938

Most of the country correspondence of the political departments from 1920 onwards can be found in FO 371. However, in some cases, the final number of the
reference may not refer to a country or subject in the FO 371 series, but may be a
supplementary number which refers to the records of the non-political departments
of the Office. A key to these is also provided in the list at the front of each index

volume. The key usually provides enough information to identify the department or subject concerned. The most relevant classes with their departmental prefixes are as follows:

FO 366   Chief Clerk's (X)

FO 950   Claims (KC)

FO 850   Communications (Y)

FO 369   Consular (K)

FO 924   Cultural Relations (LC)

FO 627   Dominions Information (U), 1922-1933

FO 930,   Information (P), 1946 onwards
FO 953

FO 370   Library (L)

FO 395   News (P)

FO 372   Treaty (T)

The full modern reference for surviving documents in these series can be identified by using the appropriate class lists. You should look for the appropriate entry in the list under the correct country, file and paper number as described above.

After 1940 the indexes to the general correspondence also include references to green papers. These are papers deemed to be of special sensitivity and which were dealt with in a separate secret registry. They are easily identifiable by the green bands running across the top of the file covers containing secret papers. Before 1940 there are separate 'green' indexes. However, not all secret papers were registered as green papers, and not all green papers were necessarily classified as secret.

For the years 1950 onwards the references in the index are in a slightly different format due to revision of the Foreign Office filing system, as the sample given on page 152 shows.

342

Indo-China.

See also FRANCE: COLONIES AND ASSOCIATED TERRITORIES.

Participation in Colombo Plan.
— See ASIA (SOUTH-EAST).

F.O.R.D. memoranda and papers on Indo-China: basic information: history, racial origin and economic potentialities; political events and organisations. FF/1015/1-4-13-18-86-90.

— Political and religious influence of Roman Catholics. FF/1781/2.

Constitutional position in French Union of Cambodia, Laos and Vietnam. FF/10317/1-25-49.

Constitutional position for the purposes of Inter-governmental Maritime Consultative Organisation (I.M.C.O.): enquiry by Ministry of Transport. FF/140/1.

— And for Safety of Life at Sea Convention. G/2/40.

Pau conference in 1950 between France, Laos, Vietnam and Cambodia: summary of proceedings: texts of conventions agreed: reports from H.M.R. Paris and H.M.R. Saigon: circulated to Cabinet (E.D.(S.A.)(51)38. FF/10317/7-11-16-17/FZ/1103/56.

Monthly political reports from H.M.R. Saigon. FF/1013/file.

Personalities reports. FH/1012/1-2-3.

Position of parties: influence of Bao Dai: cabinet changes: French attitude towards internal situation: attitude of Catholics. FF/1015/file.

National Popular Party (Dai Viet) meeting at Hanoi in December, 1950: resolution pledging military support to régime in fight against Viet Minh: text. FH/1015/2.

Future of Indo-China following transfer of power: need for strong leadership: failure of Bao Dai to rally nation: review of situation by H.M.R. Saigon. FF/1015/3.

Viet Doan party: manifesto issued by: political activities: comments of H.M.R. Saigon. FF/1015/8.

General de Lattre's concern over political situation and financial transactions of Bao Dai and leading members of the Govt.: record of

Indo-China (continued).

Than Hien Bao Quoc (Youth group for the protection of the Fatherland): assassin of General Chauson and Thai Lap Than alleged to be member: information regarding organisation. FF/1015/123-128-129.

Effect on of dissensions between General de Lattre and Vietnamese leaders: report on developments prior to General's visit to France from H.M.R., Saigon. FF/1015/125.

Civil organisation, relief and reconstruction following military operations: activities of Nguyen Van Tam in north: reports on success of. FF/1015/133-155.

Visit of Mr. Malcolm MacDonald in November: press statement on departure: text. FF/1015/142-144.

Informal visit of Mr. Malcolm MacDonald in May at invitation of General de Lattre: report from H.M.R., Saigon. FF/1052/17-19.

Mr. Malcolm MacDonald's visit to Indo-China in November. FF/1052/67-73-78.

— Record of conversation with Bao Dai on military and political situation. FF/1052/77.

Brief on situation for discussion with Mr. Casey. FF/1015/146.

Visit by Mr. Gauquié, French Ambassador, Batavia: favourable impressions of H.M.G.'s Far East policy: report from H.M.R., Djakarta. FH/1024/7.

Brief for S. of S.'s discussion with Pandit Nehru in January. FF/1052/1.

Chinese threat: General de Lattre's belief that he has backing of S. of S. in trying to avert by negotiation: comments of H.M.R., Saigon. FF/1052/2.

Attitude of Indian Govt.: Mr. Pignon's impressions following visit to New Delhi: record of conversation with H.M. Ambassador, Paris. FF/1052/3.

Military aid from U.K. and United States: French needs for reinforcements in Indo-China and difficulties in providing to be discussed by Mr. Pleven in Washington. FF/1052/4-5-6.

Likelihood of French requests for allied ground forces in Indo-China: views of Sir O. Harvey, Paris. FF/1052/79.

Index volume for 1951, showing entries under Indo-China: Military aid from UK and US. French needs for reinforcements in Indo-China and difficulties in providing, to be discussed by Mr Pleven in Washington. FF/1052/4-5-6.

The entries now run in the following order:

an initial letter or letters indicating the Foreign Office Department and sub-division;

a file number;

a paper number or a sequence of paper numbers.

The codes can again be interpreted using the keys at the front of the volume, which differ slightly from those in earlier volumes:

DEPARTMENTAL SUB-DIVISIONS CLASSIFIED ACCORDING TO TERRITORIES AND SUBJECTS, WITH THEIR RESPECTIVE INDEX LETTERS

DEPARTMENTS

A	American	K	Consular	UP	United Nations (Political)
B	Commonwealth Liaison	L	Library and Research	US	United Nations (Economic and Social)
C	German Political and Austrian Section	M	Mutual Aid	W	Western
		N	Northern	WU	Western Organisations
CR	Cultural Relations	P	Information, Policy and News	X	Conference and Supply, Finance, Personnel, and Establishment and Organisation
E	Eastern	PR	Information Research		
F	Far Eastern and South-East Asia	Q	Security		
G	General	R	Southern	Y	Communications
H	Claims	T	Treaty	Z	Permanent Under-Secretary's Department
J	African	UE	Economic Relations		

INDEX LETTERS ARRANGED ALPHABETICALLY

A	American: General	CR	Cultural Relations: General	FT	Tibet
AA	Argentina	CRA	Administration	FZ	South-East Asia (Miscellaneous)
AB	Brazil	CRE	Examinations		
AC	Chile	CRL	Cultural Activities	G	General: Miscellaneous
AD	Dominican Republic			GA	Civil Aviation
AE	Ecuador	E	Eastern: General	GE	Atomic Energy
AF	Peru	EA	Arabia	GM	Postal Services
AG	Guatemala	EE	Palestine	GR	International Rivers
AH	Honduras	EL	Lebanon	GS	Shipping
AK	Cuba	EP	Persia	GT	Telecommunications
AL	Colombia	EQ	Iraq	GY	Communications and Transit
AM	Mexico	ER	Israel		
AN	Nicaragua	ES	Saudi Arabia	H	Claims: General
AP	Panama	ET	Jordan	HG*	Geographical
AR	Costa Rica	EY	Syria		
AS	Salvador			J	African: General
AT	Hayti	F	Far Eastern: General	JA	Ethiopia
AU	United States	FA	Afghanistan	JB	Belgian Congo
AV	Venezuela	FB	Burma	JE	Egypt and Sudan
AW	Uruguay	FC	China	JF	French Africa
AX	Bolivia	FD	New Hebrides	JL	Liberia
AY	Paraguay	FE	Portuguese Timor	JM	Morocco
		FF	French Indo-China	JP	Portuguese Africa
B	Commonwealth Liaison	FG	French Oceania	JT	Italian Colonies
		FH	Indonesia		
C	German Political Internal, and Austrian Section	FJ	Japan	K	Consular: General
		FK	Korea	KE	Estates
CD	German Education	FL	India and Pakistan	KG*	Geographical
CE	German Commercial Relations and Industry	FN	Nepal	KL	Legalisation of Documents
		FP	Philippines		
CF	German Finance	FR	South Pacific Commission	L	Library: Miscellaneous
CJ	German General Economic	FS	Siam	LF	Facilities

* The " Geographical " sub-divisions of the papers of Consular, Claims and Information Policy Departments (*i.e.*, KG, HG, PG), are further classified by countries, each country being indicated by the first three figures of the file number. A list of countries and their respective code numbers are given on page (v).

Page from volume of index for 1951, with key.

In this case the first letters identify the department (Far Eastern, South East Asia) and the country, (French Indo-China). The second letter usually refers to a departmental sub-division. In this example the second letter denotes French Indo-China. The first number (1052) is now the file number, and the other numbers (4-5-6) are those of the papers on the file.

Use the lists to find the ordering reference as described above, by looking through the relevant FO 371 volume, in this case for the year 1951, and the departmental heading and code for Far East, French Indo-China. Trace the file number in the right hand column. In this example the full reference for ordering the original document is FO 371/92424. The list indicates that the first nineteen pages are in this file.

	Reference	1951 :	FO 371
	FO 371	Description	Files
This margin not to be used.		French Indo-China (FF) – contd	
	92422	Effect of Korean situation and impending cease-fire on situation in Indo-China; hopes for cessation of Indo-Chinese war and attempts to start peace talks with Ho Chi Minh	10381
	92423	Inability of British to lend French an aircraft carrier during 1951; loan of an American carrier instead	1051
	92424	Reports and briefs concerning visit of Malcolm MacDonald Commissioner-General for South East Asia first to the UK and then to Indo-China where he met King Bao Dai; visit of Vietnamese President of the Council Tran Van Huu to London; Vietnamese press reaction to British change of government	1052 (pp to 19)

FO 371   Sample page of list covering french Indo-China, 1951

Once the document has been received you should trace the file and paper by looking at the file covers in the volume or bundle for the relevant number.

Readers should note that there is no centralised index after 1951. The only means of reference to the Foreign Office general correspondence after this date is by the class lists which may be indexed or in the process of being listed in more detail by the PRO. As another complication the new filing system was introduced by the Refugees Department and the German section only in 1951. References to papers from these two departments continue to be given under the older format in 1950.

Some Foreign Office records have been published in printed form. Transcriptions of selected documents, with file references, can be found in: *Documents on British Foreign Policy, 1919-1939*, edited by E L Woodward, Rohan Butler, et al (three series, London, HMSO, 1947-, continuing) and *Documents on British Policy Overseas, 1945-1950*, edited by Rohan Butler, et al (two series, London, HMSO, 1984-1991, continuing) These provide a useful additional source of references and copies are available in the Reference Room at Kew.

18.5 Using Embassy and Consular Registers and Indexes

Embassies and consulates produced several different types of correspondence:

> that with the Foreign Office;

> that with other British consular posts in the country concerned;

> that with the central or local government of the country in which the mission was situated;

> and that with individuals and organistions resident in or with interests in the country concerned.

This material is arranged in individual classes of general consular correspondence, with associated letter books and registers of correspondence. Indexes for the registers of correspondence may occasionally survive. There are usually individual classes of records for consulates, which sometimes also have their own registers and indexes which were kept in a similar manner to those of the embassies although fewer of these have survived.

To find a specific record relating to a subject or person, you will need to look first at the 'FO Index' binder situated at the front of the set of FO class lists in the Reference Room. Where the registers and correspondence survive, the registers can be used to find individual papers relating to a particular subject or event. A sample page, showing classes of records relating to Spain, is given below:

```
SPAIN
   General Correspondence                          FO 72
   Confidential Print                              FO 425, FO 498
   Embassy and Consular Archives:  Correspondence  FO 185
        "      "      "       "  : Letter Books    FO 186
        "      "      "       "  : Registers of    FO 187
                                     Correspondence
        "      "      "       "  : Miscellanea     FO 227
   Consulates:  Balearic Islands                   FO 214
        "     : Barcelona:  Correspondence         FO 637
        "     :    "     : Letter Books            FO 638
        "     :    "     : Miscellanea             FO 639
```

Sample page of FO index, showing embassy and consular record classes for Spain.

There are different classes for the records of the consulates themselves, for the consular material sent and received by the embassy with oversight of the consulates, and for the registers kept centrally and locally. The FO index does not give a date range for the record classes but you can find this out from the class information given in part 2 of the *Current Guide* and the lists themselves.

You will now need to refer to the class list for the registers concerned. The general registers refer to embassy and consular correspondence to and from the consuls, to and from the Foreign Office and to and from the government of the country to which the embassy and consulates were accredited. The Foreign Office correspondence may be divided into commercial and political. It is often necessary to look under some or all of these types of registers to trace all the papers relating to a particular subject or event.

The example below shows part of the list for FO 187, the Embassy and Consular Archives (Spain) Registers of Correspondence. In this case, the register of correspondence to the Foreign Office, 1836 to 1843 has been selected as an example (FO 187/12).

FO 187	Date	Description
1	1810 Mar.-1812 May	To Foreign Office.
2	1812 May-1815 Aug.	" "
3	1815 Aug.-1828 Dec.	Spanish Government.
4	1816 Dec.-1819 Dec.	To Foreign Office.
5	1820-1829	" "
6	1822-1839	From Spanish Government.
7	1822 Aug.-1841 Aug.	From Foreign Office.
8	1829 Jan.-1844 Aug.	To Spanish Government.
9	1830-1836 June	To Foreign Office.
10	1834-1852 Oct.	To Consuls and Miscellaneous.
11	1834-1853	" "
12	1836 July-1843 Dec.	To Foreign Office.
13	1840-1867	From Spanish Government.

This margin not to be used.

Sample of **FO 187** list showing FO 187/12 marked on the list as an example.

Order the register or registers you require using the reference given in the left hand column in the usual way. Once your document arrives, it will provide you with the information as shown below. As an example, supposing that you were following the course of Anglo-Spanish relations in the 1830s, the attitude of the Queen Regent is likely to be of interest. In this register the report of an interview with the Regent has been used.

FO 187/12   Pages of register from 1836, showing a report of an interview with the Queen Regent, dated 31 July, sent to Lord Palmerston on 1 August by Mr Villiers (no. 186).

Once you have located an entry of interest, the most important details to note are the date of the despatch, its contents or subject, who it is to and the number of the despatch, which is given here on the third column on the left hand page (A number at the end of the description on the right hand page indicates that there is further correspondence, which can be traced by searching the despatch number column on the left hand side for the appropriate number). In order to trace this report in the correspondence you would note the date (31 July), that the despatch is to Lord Palmerston and the number of the despatch (186).

Once you have this information you should consult the FO index again to find out which class contains the correspondence. In this case, the most obvious class is FO 185. Look at the class list in the first instance for the date, in this case July 1836.

F.O. 185.			
CORRESPONDENCE.—continued.			
55	1815.	Consuls.	
56	1815.	,,	
57	1815.	Claims.	
58	1815.	Various.	
59	1816.	From Foreign Office.	
60	1816.	To ,,	
61	1816.	Spanish Government.	
62	1816.	From British ministers, Naval officers, and Gibraltar.	
63	1816.	Consuls.	
64	1816.	,,	
65	1816.	Various.	
66	1817.	From Foreign Office.	
67	1817.	To ,, / From British ministers.	
68	1817.	Spanish Government. / From Gibraltar.	
69	1817.	Consuls.	
70	1817.	Various.	
71	1818.	From Foreign Office.	
72	1818.	To ,, / Spanish Government.	
73	1818.	From British ministers and Gibraltar.	
74	1818.	Consuls and various.	
75	1819.	Foreign Office.	
76	1819.	British ministers and Spanish Government.	
77	1819.	Gibraltar and Consuls.	
78	1819.	Various.	
79	1820.	From Foreign Office.	
80	1820.	To ,,	
81	1820.	British ministers and Spanish Government.	
82	1820.	Consuls and various.	
83	1821.	Foreign Office.	
84	1821.	British ministers and Spanish Government.	
85	1821.	Consuls and various.	
86	1822 Jan.–Oct.	From Foreign Office.	
87	1822 Nov.–Dec.	,,	
88	1822.	To Foreign Office.	
89	1822.	British ministers and Spanish Govern-	

F.O. 185.			
CORRESPONDENCE—continued.			
127	1830.	Consuls.	
128	1830.	Various.	
129	1831.	Foreign Office.	
130	1831.	Consuls.	
131	1831.	Spanish Government and various.	
132	1832.	From Foreign Office.	
133	1832.	To ,,	
134	1832.	Spanish Government. / To Consuls and various.	
135	1832 Jan.–Aug.	From Consuls and various.	
136	1832 Sept.–Dec.	,,	
137	1833.	From Foreign Office.	
138	1833.	To ,,	
139	1833.	Foreign Office (slave trade).	
140	1833.	Spanish Government.	
141	1833 Jan.–Aug.	From Consuls and various.	
142	1833 Sept.–Dec.	,, / To ,,	
143	1833–1836.	Claims and special cases.	
144	1833–1836.	,,	
145	1834.	From Foreign Office.	
146	1834.	To ,,	
147	1834.	Spanish Government. / To Consuls and various.	
148	1834 Jan.–July.	From Consuls and various.	
149	1834 Aug.–Dec.	,,	
150	1835 Jan.–Oct.	From Foreign Office.	
151	1835 Oct.–Dec. / 1835.	From Foreign Office (slave trade).	
152	1835.	To Foreign Office.	
153	1835.	Spanish Government.	
154	1835.	Consuls.	
155	1835.	Various.	
156	1836 Jan.–Sept.	From Foreign Office.	
157	1836 Oct.–Dec. / 1836.	From Foreign Office (slave trade).	
158	1836.	To Foreign Office.	
159	1836.	Spanish Government.	
160	1836.	Consuls and various.	
161	1836.	,,	
162	1837 Jan.–June.	From Foreign Office.	
163	1837 July–Dec.	,,	

FO 185 class list, covering 1836

Since the correspondence is directed to the Foreign Office, the most likely reference is FO 185/158. Once you have ordered this document, you should look through the volume or bundles for the despatch number (186), and date, and any other details which fit those that you have noted from the register. The identifying features can be seen in the example given below:

(copy)

Nº 186.

St. Ildefonso July 31st 1836 —

My Lord,

On the 29th Instant I had the honour of being received by the Queen Regent —

H.M., in adverting to the alarm which had been created here on the 27th — Instant by the approval of the Carlists, said that She had not determined upon leaving St. Ildefonso in so precipitate a manner from any personal fear for Herself or in ignorance of the evil consequences which such a step would have produced : but that, having received

To The Viscount Palmerston
&c &c &c —

1836
St. Ildefonso July 31st —
Mr. Villiers —
Nº 186 —

By Courier McMartin —
Interview with the
Queen Regent —

P.2.L.6 —

Copy of endorsement of **FO 185/158** and first page of despatch.
From Villiers, July 31 1836 (No. 186)

159

In the case of correspondence to and from the Foreign Office, duplicate or original copies of the correspondence can be found amongst the general Foreign Office correspondence. In this case the relevant class is FO 72. The sample page of the list for this class shows how this material can be identified, provided that you know the name of the consul or ambassador sending the despatch.

SPAIN—*continued.*

F.O. 72.		
400	1832	Jan.–May. Domestic various.
401	1832	June–Dec. ,,
402	1830–1834.	W. John McLeay.
403	1832	Dec. 1834 March. Sir Stratford Canning.
404	1833	Apr–May. ,, ,,
405	1833	Jan.–Sept. To H. U. Addington.
406	1833	Sept.–Dec. To George Villiers.
407	1833	Jan. Feb. From H. U. Addington.
408	1833	March–April. ,,
409	1833	May–June 27 ,,
410	1833	June 29 Aug. 8. ,,
411	1833	Aug. 10–Sept. ,,
412	1833	Sept.–Oct. From George Villiers.
413	1833	Nov.–Dec. ,,
414	1833	Consuls John Clark, John Crispin, Benito Santos, William Mark, J. M. Brackenbury, Charles Chamberlain, Matthew Carter.
415	1833.	Consuls Jasper Waring, James Annesley, John Montagu, Lewis C. Hargrave, Richard Bartlett, Charles David Tolme, John Hardy.
416	1833.	Lord William Hervey, Newton Saville Scott, and John M. P. Grant, Foreign and Consular Domestic.
417	1833.	Domestic, M. Cordoba, Chevalier de Vial.
418	1833.	Domestic various.
419	1834.	To George Villiers.
420	1834	Jan.–Feb. From George Villiers.
421	1834	March. ,,
422	1834	April. ,,
423	1834	May–June. ,,
424	1834	July. ,,
425	1834	Aug. 2–16. ,,
426	1834	Aug. 23–Sept. 15. ,,
427	1834	Sept. 16–Nov. 2. ,,
428	1834	Nov. 2–Dec. ,,
429	1834.	Newton Saville Scott, L. C. Otway, Consuls John Clark, John Crispin, J. M. Brackenbury, William Mark, Matthew Carter.
430	1834.	Consuls Jasper Waring, James Annesley, John Montagu, Lewis C. Hargrave, Richard Bartlett.
431	1834.	Consuls Charles David Tolmé, John Hardy, John Clark. Foreign various and Consular Domestic.
432	1834	June. J. Backhouse, Don Carlos. [A]
433	1834	Jan.–July. Domestic, M. de Vial and Marquis de Miraflores.
434	1834	Aug.–Dec. Domestic, M. de Vial, Marquis de Miraflores, and M. de Jabat.
435	1834	Jan.–June. Domestic various.
436	1834	July–Sept. ,,
437	1834	Sept.–Oct. ,,
438	1834	Nov.–Dec. ,,
439	1835.	To George Villiers.
440	1835	Jan.–Feb. From George Villiers
441	1835	March–April. ,,
442	1835	May–June. ,,
443	1835	July Aug. ,,
444	1835	Sept.–Oct. ,,
445	1835	Nov.–Dec. ,,
446	1834–1835.	Colonel Carador, Lord Eliot,

F.O. 72.		
455	1835	Oct.–Dec. Domestic various.
456	1836.	To George Villiers.
457	1836	Jan.–Feb. From George Villiers.
458	1836	March–April. ,,
459	1836	May–June. ,,
460	1836	July–Aug. 27. ,,
461	1836	Aug. 30 Oct. 8. ,,
462	1836	Oct. 13–Nov. 12. ,,
463	1836	Nov. 19–Dec. ,,
464	1836.	Lieut.-Col. W. Wylde, Lieut.-Gen. de Lacy Evans.
465	1836.	Loftus Otway, Consuls John Clark, J. M. Brackenbury.
466	1836.	Consul William Mark.
467	1836.	Consuls Matthew Carter, Jasper Waring, James Annesley, James Hargrave, Richard Bartlett, Lewis C. Hamilton.
468	1836.	Consuls Charles David Tolmé, John Hardy.
469	1836.	Foreign and Consular Domestic.
470	1836.	Domestic, Ignacio Jabat, Juan Cimenez de Sandovai, Manuel Maria de Aguila.
471	1836	Jan.–March. Domestic various.
472	1836	April–June. ,,
473	1836	July–Sept. ,,
474	1836	Oct.–Dec. ,,
475	1837	Jan.–June. To George Villiers.
476	1837	July–Dec. ,,
477	1837	Jan. From ,,
478	1837	Feb.–March. ,,
479	1837	April–May 20. ,,
480	1837	May 28–June. ,,
481	1837	July 1–22. ,,
482	1837	July 29–Aug. ,,
483	1837	Sept.–Oct. 14. ,,
484	1837	Oct. 21–Nov. ,,
485	1837	Dec. ,,
486	1837.	Lieut.-Col. W. Wylde, Colonel J. Lacy, Lieutenant J. Lynn, Lieutenant George E. Turner.
487	1837.	Consul J. M. Brackenbury.
488	1837.	Consuls John Clark, John Crispin, Leopold Menendez, William Penrose Mark, Matthew Carter, Jasper Waring.
489	1837.	Consuls James Annesley, Richard Bartlett, Charles David Tolmé, John Hardy.
490	1837.	Foreign various and Consular Domestic.
491	1837	Jan.–June. Domestic, M. Manuel Maria de Aguilar.
492	1837	July–Dec. ,, ,,
493	1837	Jan.–April. Domestic various.
494	1837	May–June. ,,
495	1837	July–Aug. ,,
496	1837	Sept.–Oct. 21. ,,
497	1837	Oct. 24–Nov. ,,
498	1837	Dec. ,,
499	1838	Jan.–May. To George Villiers.
500	1838	June–Dec. To George Villiers and Lord William Hervey.
501	1838	Jan.–Feb. 10. From George Villiers
502	1838	Feb. 12–March 24. ,,

FO 72 Sample page from the list

The reference to be noted here is FO 72/460. Once the document has been ordered and has arrived you should be able to find the letter by using the despatch number and date given in the register.

This example has dealt with correspondence to and from the embassy to the Foreign Office and the receiving government. It is possible, however, to trace that between the embassy and the consulates. If you consult one of the general registers you will find that they are divided into cuts for various types of correspondence. The general registers are marked in the list as in the illustration below, although there may also be registers dealing with consular and miscellaneous subjects.

	EMBASSY AND CONSULAR ARCHIVES: SPAIN: REGISTERS		
Reference			FO 187
FO 187	Date	Description	
29	1867-1871	Consuls and Miscellaneous.	
30	1871 Feb.-1873 Oct.	General.	
31	1873 Oct.-1875 Dec.	"	
32	1876 Jan.-1879 Feb.	"	
33	1879 Mar.-1883 Dec.	"	
34	1884-1887	"	
35	1888-1892	"	
36	1892 July-1894	"	
37	1895-1897	"	
38	1898	"	
39	1899-1900	"	
40	1901	"	
41	1902-1904	"	
42	1905-1907	"	
43	1908-1910	"	
44	1911-1913	"	

This margin not to be used.

FO 187 Sample page of list, with piece 39 highlighted.

Using the general register for 1899 to 1900 a typical page showing entries under
the consular cut looks like this:

FO 187/39 In this case, a request to the consul for a new list of foreign vessels has been
used as an example, giving the references by column, 39 Peninsula Consuls, 3 April
New list, 71 C 83 FO. The facing page shows related incoming correspondence.

The left hand side refers to correspondence from the consuls and the right hand side to correspondence to the consuls. Each page includes information which enables the reader to see the relationship between both sides of the correspondence. In this example, supposing that you were interested in naval intelligence on Spanish ships, the entry for 3 April highlighted on the diagram on the 'to consuls' page may be relevant. Looking at the information on this line, the 39 provides the registry number, while other columns provide circulation details, date and subject. The numbers at the end of the subject entry are cross- referencing codes for the register. In this case '71 C' refers to number 71 of the 'from consuls' page and the corresponding entry can be found on the left hand page of the register. '83 FO' refers to number 83 in the Foreign Office correspondence cut which can be traced in the appropriate part of the register.

Once an entry of interest has been identified you should refer to the class list which contains material described in the register. In this case the appropriate class is FO 185, Spain: Embassy and Consular Archives Correspondence.

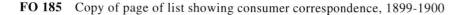

```
                        SPAIN
                    CORRESPONDENCE

    Reference      Date                    Description

    F.O.185

       887         1898      To Miscellaneous.

       888         1899      From Foreign Office.

       889         1899        "      "      "

       890         1899        "      "      "

       891         1899      To     "      "

       892         1899        "      "      "

       893         1899        "      "      "

       894         1899      From   "      "   (Commercial).

       895         1899        "      "      "           "

       896         1899        "      "      "           "

       897         1899      To Foreign Office (Commercial).

       898         1899        "      "      "           "

       899         1899      From Spanish Government.

       900         1899      To     "      "

       901         1899      From Consuls.

       902         1899        "      "

       903         1899        "      "

       904         1899      To     "
```

FO 185   Copy of page of list showing consumer correspondence, 1899-1900

Look for the most appropriate heading in the right hand description column of the list. In this case the right document reference is FO 185/904 - To Consuls, 1899. If you wished to trace the other part of the correspondence, that from the consuls in 1899 you would need to order FO 185/901-903. Once the document arrives you will need to search through the volume or papers looking for the registry number and the date. In this case the reply to the consuls dated 3 April can be most conveniently identified using the date:

New list of Foreign War Vessel   N .

Madrid
April 3/99

Mr Adam
to
Peninsular Consuls

Sir,

With reference to Mr Barclay's despatch of Mar 5th 1898 I transmit herewith a new list of Foreign vessels of which the Lords Commissioners of the admiralty desire to obtain photographs.

I request that you will endeavour to obtain photographs of the ships now specified, under the conditions as to expenses already explained, and that you will cancel and destroy the former list .

39 Consuls

Page of **FO 185/904**   Mr Adam to the peninsular consuls, April 3, transmitting an Admiralty request for photographs of specified foreign vessels

This section has looked at a very simple search, using a limited number of classes in a particular area. There may be variations in other classes, but you should approach all of them using the general principles outlined above.

It should be noted that embassy and consular material can be duplicated amongst the general correspondence, as drafts to missions were usually kept, and much internal consular material was copied to the Foreign Office for information. If a document cannot be traced through these records it is always worth checking the relevant general correspondence class. Since the records of embassies and consulates are arranged under the country exercising sovereignity at a particular time, material relating to the same consulate may appear in totally separate record classes at different dates.

There may also be a separate miscellaneous class of records relating to a particular embassy or consulate. Their contents are extremely varied, but as a general guide they can contain memoranda, reports, (statistical, political, economic or cultural), copies of treaties and conventions, circulars, claims and concessions, confidential print, and material concerning commissions and tribunals.

19. Further Reading

The basic guide to the records of the Foreign Office is still PRO Handbook 13, *The Records of the Foreign Office 1782-1939* (London, 1969). This book is now out of print, but reference copies are available at both Kew and Chancery Lane.

Medieval Diplomacy

P Chaplais   *English Medieval Diplomatic Practice* 2 volumes (London, 1982)

G P Cuttino   *English Diplomatic Administration 1259-1339* (Oxford, 1971)

J Ferguson   *English Diplomacy 1422-1461* (Oxford, 1972)

M C Hill   *The King's Messengers, 1199-1377* (London, 1961)

D E Queller   *The Office of Ambassador in the Middle Ages* (Princeton, 1967)

Early Modern Diplomacy and the State Papers

J Y Akeman (ed),   *Secret Service Expenses of Charles II and James II*, Camden Society, 1851

G E Aylmer   *The King's Servants: the Civil Servants of Charles I, 1625-1642* (London, 1961)
The State's Servants: the Civil Service of the English Republic (London/Boston, 1973)

J Black   'Eighteenth Century Intercepted Despatches', *Journal of the Society of Archivists*, volume 11, no. 4, October 1990

K L Ellis   'British Communication and Diplomacy in the 18th century', *Bulletin of the Institute of Historical Research* (1958)

H M G Evans   *The Principal Secretary of State 1558-1680* (Manchester, 1923)

P Fraser   *The Intelligence of the Secretaries of State and Their Monopoly of Licensed News, 1660-1688* (Cambridge University Press, 1956)

D B Horn   *The British Diplomatic Service 1689-1789* (Oxford 1961)

'The Diplomatic Experiences of Secretaries of State, 1660-1852', *History*, 1956.

'The Machinery for the Conduct of British Foreign Policy in the 18th century', *Journal of the Society of Archivists*, 3, 1967

D Kynaston   *The Secretary of State* (Lavenham, 1978)

P S Lachs   *The Diplomatic Corps under Charles II and James II* (New Jersey, 1966)

J C Sainty   *Officials of the Secretaries of State, 1681-1782* (London, 1932)

M A Thomson   *The Secretaries of State, 1681-1782* (Oxford 1932)

A C Wood   *A History of the Levant Company* (OUP, 1935)

The Foreign Office and the Foreign Secretary

R Bullen (ed)   *The Foreign Office, 1782-1982* (Maryland, USA, 1984)

V Cromwell   'The FCO', in Z Steiner, ed. *Times Survey of the Foreign Ministries of the World* (London, 1982)

J Dickie   *Inside the Foreign Office* (London, 1992)

N Hart   *The Foreign Secretary* (Lavenham, 1987)

E Hertslet, Sir   *Recollections of the Old Foreign Office* (London, 1901)

R Jones   *The Nineteenth Century Foreign Office: A Study in Administrative History* (London, 1971)

R Langhorne   'The Foreign Office before 1914', *Historical Journal,* 16 (1973)

G Moorhouse   *The Diplomats* (London, 1977)

Z Steiner   *The Foreign Office and Foreign Policy 1898-1914* (Cambridge, 1969)

Z Steiner and M Dockrill   'Foreign Office Reforms 1919-1921', *Historical Journal*, 17 (1974)

Lord Strang   *The Foreign Office* (London, 1955)

J Tilley and S Gaselee   *The Foreign Office* (London, 1933)

The Diplomatic and Consular Services

S T Bindoff   'The Unreformed Diplomatic Service 1812-1860' *Transactions of the Royal Historical Society,* 18 (1935)

R Jones   *The British Diplomatic Service 1815-1914* (Gerrards Cross, 1983)

D C M Platt   *The Cinderella Service: British Consuls since 1825* (London, 1971)

G Yeo   *The British Overseas* (Guildhall Library Guide 2, 2nd. ed. London, 1988)

Modern Foreign Policy

K Bourne   *The Foreign Policy of Victorian England 1830-1902* (London, 1970)

M Chamberlain   *British Foreign Policy in the Age of Palmerston* (London, 1980)

F Gosses   *The Management of British Foreign Policy before the First World War* (Leiden, 1948)

P Hayes   *Modern British Foreign Policy: the Nineteenth Century, 1815-1888* (London, 1975
Modern British Foreign Policy: the Twentieth Century, 1888-1939 (London, 1978)

P Kennedy   *The Realities behind Diplomacy* (Fontana, 1981)

P Langford   *Modern British Foreign Policy: the Eighteenth Century, 1688-1815,* (London, 1976)

C R Middleton   *The Administration of British Foreign Policy, 1782-1846* (Durham USA, 1977)

A W Ward and G P Gooch, (eds)   *Cambridge History of British Foreign Policy 1783-1919,* 3 volumes (Cambridge, 1922-1923)

20. Appendixes

20.1 Geographical Index to the State Papers Foreign

'Geographical' in the context of international affairs in the seventeenth and eighteenth centuries, is anything but a precise term, and the following is included as a general guide only.

Algiers	See Barbary States
Barbary States	SP 71, SP 102, SP 103, SP 108 SP 110
Denmark	SP 75, SP 100, SP 101, SP 102, SP 103, SP 104, SP 105, SP 108, SP 110, SP 115
Dunkirk	SP 76, SP 105
Flanders	SP 77, SP 83, SP 101, SP 103, SP 104, SP 105
France	SP 78, SP 100, SP 101, SP 102, SP 103, SP 105, SP 108.
Genoa	SP 79, SP 101, SP 108
Germany (Empire) and Hungary	SP 80, SP 100, SP 101, SP 102, SP 103, SP 105, SP 108, SP 110, SP 118
Germany (States)	SP 81, SP 100, SP 102, SP 103, SP 104, SP 105, SP 108
Hamburg and Hanse Towns	SP 82, SP 101, SP 102, SP 103, SP 104, SP 108
Holland	SP 83, SP 84, SP 100, SP 101, SP 102, SP 103, SP 104, SP 108
Italian States	SP 85, SP 100, SP 101, SP 102, SP 103, SP 104
Malta	SP 86
Mantua	See Italian States

Milan	See Italian States
Modena	SP 108
Morocco	See Barbary States
Naples	See Sicily
Parma	See Italian states
Persia	SP 102
Poland	SP 88, SP 100, SP 102, SP 103, SP 104, SP 108, SP 122
Portugal	SP 89, SP 100, SP 101, SP 102, SP 103, SP 104, SP 108, SP 110, SP 123
Prussia	SP 90, SP 100, SP 102, SP 103, SP 104, SP 108, SP 110
Rome	See Italian States
Russia	SP 91, SP 100, SP 102, SP 103, SP 104, SP 108, SP 124
Sardinia	See Savoy
Savoy	SP 92, SP 102, SP 108
Sicily	SP 93, SP 102
Spain	SP 94, SP 100, SP 101, SP 102, SP 103, SP 104, SP 108, SP 110, SP 125
Sweden	SP 95, SP 100, SP 101, SP 102, SP 103, SP 104, SP 108, SP 126
Switzerland	SP 96, SP 101, SP 102, SP 104, SP 108, SP 127

Tripoli	See Barbary States
Tunis	See Barbary States
Turkey	SP 97, SP 102, SP 103, SP 104, SP 105, SP 108, SP 110
Tuscany	SP 98, SP 101, SP 102, SP 105
Vatican	see Italian states
Venice	SP 99, SP 104, SP 105

20.2 Overlaps Between State Paper And Foreign Office Classes

Although 1782 is technically the date when the Foreign Office came into existence, there are records within Foreign Office classes which are relevant to the history of diplomatic affairs when they still came under the dual control of the two secretaries of state. Some of classes listed below do contain genuinely contemporary material, but sometimes the documents referred to may be catalogues or copies of documents made at a much later date. The available lists do not always distinguish such documents.

The classes can be listed as follows:

FO 3	General Correspondence before 1906 Algiers, 1760-1850. See also SP 71, Barbary States
FO 28	General Correspondence before 1906 Genoa, 1776-1803. See also SP 79, Genoa
FO 41	General Correspondence before 1906 East India, 1776-1797
FO 42	General Correspondence before 1906 Ionian Islands, 1778-1820
FO 57	General Correspondence before 1906 Nice, 1777-1800
FO 76	General Correspondence before 1906 Tripoli, 1756-1837
FO 77	General Correspondence before 1906 Tunis, Series I, 1770-1837

FO 78	General Correspondence before 1906 Turkey, 1780-1905
FO 79	General Correspondence before 1906 Tuscany, 1780-1860
FO 83	General Correspondence, Great Britain and General, 1745-1967
FO 90	King's Letter Books 1710-1828 - continues SP 104
FO 93	Protocols of Treaties, 1695-1989
FO 95	Miscellanea This includes correspondence relating to Algiers, 1791-1801, with copies 1698-1809 and 1695-1816; Tripoli, 1675-1818; Tunis, 1699-1621; correspondence of papers of Comte d'Avaux, 1672-c.1701; papers covering Spanish affairs, 1777-1789; Portugal and Brazil; [1772]; Entry books of treaties, ratifications, etc, 1639-1834
FO 96	Miscellanea Series II, c.1700-1951
FO 113	Embassy and Consular Archives Algiers Miscellanea, 1567-1914
FO 160	Embassy and Consular Archives Libya (Tripoli) Letter books and Correspondence, 1700-1948
FO 161 ous,	Embassy and Consular Archives Libya (Tripoli) Miscellane- c.1742-1951
FO 227	Embassy and Consular Archives Spain Miscellanea, 1704-1914
FO 233	Embassy and Consular Archives China Miscellanea, 1727-1951
FO 261	Embassy and Consular Archives Turkey Additional, 1776-1794
FO 323	Miscellaneous Private Collections, 1636-1887. Includes accounts of fees and disbursements, 1710-12, during Bolingbroke's Secretaryship
FO 332	Embassy and Consular Archives Seville, 1623-1948
FO 335	Embassy and Consular Archives Tunisia, (Tunis) 1669-1911
FO 339	Embassy and Consular Archives Tunisia (Tunis) Miscellanea, 1675-1936

FO 366	Chief Clerk's Department Archives, 1719-1959
FO 414	Confidential Print North America, 1711-1941
FO 425	Confidential Print Western Europe, 1769-1956
FO 602	Embassy and Consular Archives Turkey, (Basra) 1761-1914
FO 639	Embassy and Consular Archives Spain, Barcelona, 1775-1922
FO 677	Embassy and Consular Archives China, supplementary, Trade, 1759-1874
FO 722	Embassy and Consular Archives Spain, Canary Islands, 1764-1931
FO 811	Embassy and Consular Archives Portugal, Funchal Correspondence, 1750-1930
FO 861	Embassy and Consular Archives Aleppo, c. 1745-1956
FO 931	Kwantung Provincial Archives, 1765-1857 (captured during Arrow war)
SP 44	Secretaries of State: State Papers: Entry Books, 1661-1828
SP 45	State Papers Domestic, Various, Edward VI-1862
SP 46	State Papers Domestic, Supplementary, 1361-1829
SP 71	State Papers Foreign, Barbary States, 1577-1787
SP 81	State Papers Foreign, Germany, States, 1577-1784
SP 109	State Papers Foreign, Various, 1665-1788
SP 110	State Papers Foreign, Supplementary, 1616-1871
SP 112	Maps, c. 1617-c. 1837
SP 118	State Papers: Gazettes and Pamphlets: Holy Roman Empire, 1663-1784
SP 119	State Papers: Gazettes and Pamphlets: United Provinces of the Netherlands, 1664-1784

20.3 Glossary of Diplomatic Terms

The following terms have been used widely in the conduct of diplomacy and in the records produced as a result. In the very modern period economic terminology is used more frequently. A glossary which includes such terms is available in R G Feltham, *Diplomatic Handbook* (Longman, 5th edition, 1988)

Accord

An agreement concerning matters of international concern which do not merit a formal convention or treaty.

Acte Finale

At the end of a conference a summary of subject matter, discussions, or decisions taken may be drawn up. This formal document may also be called an *acte* or protocol or *proces verbal final.*

Agrément

When a government wishes to accredit a representative to another state, an informal enquiry is made of the government concerned as to the proposed representative's acceptability. This takes place before the formal request (agrément) is made.

Attaché

A specialist attached to a mission for particular duties. Initially attachés were military, naval, or air force representatives, but in the more modern period specialists can include economists or those specialising in social studies.

Bout de Papier

A 'piece of paper' containing a factual account of a conversation. It has no date, courtesies, official stamp or signature.

Capitulations

These were privileges (chiefly legal, religious and commercial) granted to resident English communities in foreign countries, for example such non-Christian states as the Ottoman Empire, and China. Together, these immunities comprised what was known as the Capitulatory System and were usually administered by the consular representatives of the Levant and China services. By the twentieth century, due to the level of abuse, these grants were repudiated by the national states involved.

Casus belli

An act committed by one power against another which is seen by that state as an occasion for war.

Casus foederis

An act or occurrence which activates a treaty of alliance and which involves another power being called upon to offer assistance.

Chargé d'affaires

The diplomatic officer acting on behalf of the head of the mission during his or her absence. Usually this is the next senior officer. They may be termed *en titre* if the government has no intention of appointing a replacement or *ad interim* if the appointment is temporary.

Commission Rogotoire

A commission for the hearing of evidence in foreign or colonial countries in cases involving British courts of law or subjects. They could also be issued to consuls.

Consular Commission

The written authority sent to the recipient government showing the name, rank, and district of the proposed consular official. If acceptable, the receiving government issues an exequatur or agrément. See Exequatur.

Convention

A secondary form of treaty which is signed between representatives of governments rather than the heads of state.

Counsellor

The senior secretary of the embassy or legation, who acts as head of mission in the absence of the ambassador. See Chargé d'affaires.

Credentials

When a representative is appointed to a post he or she is supplied with letters of credence which are signed by the head of state. When an embassy or mission is terminated the representative is presented with recredentials by the foreign government concerned.

Demarche

There is no standard translation of this term. It usually refers to the making of a representation or approach from one state to another. It can be used to describe approaches of various urgency or seriousness.

En clair

Telegrams between the Foreign Office and representatives abroad can be sent in two ways: in cipher or in ordinary English. The latter is referred to as being 'en clair'.

Envoy Extraordinary

In the early history of diplomacy there was a distinction between envoys extraordinary (for special missions) and ordinary (resident), which reflected the extent of their powers to negotiate. In the modern period all ambassadors are appointed as envoys extraordinary.

Exequatur

The official recognition of a consul or commercial agent by the government to which they are accredited and their authority to perform the stated duties.

Extraterritoriality

Another term to describe the system of privileges or jurisdiction over nationals held by a foreign community abroad, for example the convention that an embassy building is held to be the territory of the foreign power concerned.

Full Powers

These are granted by the head of state to a negotiator before the signing of a formal treaty. If the envoy is signing a convention the full powers are issued under the signature of the secretary of state.

Memoire

A memorandum of varying length which is more informal than a note or demarche and which has no introduction. The memoire may not be signed in which case it is known as a *pour-memoire*. The *aide-memoire* is a short memorandum handed by an ambassador to the foreign secretary at the end of an interview, and can also be an informal summary drawn up by foreign officials. The *aide-memoire* may also be given by British representatives abroad to the foreign minister of the power concerned. Although dated, it does not contain official courtesies, address or signature.

Memorandum

A short diplomatic communication. Also refers to a written Foreign Office summary on a particular subject or policy.

Mise en demeure

A demand made upon one government by another which produces a 'yes' or 'no' situation rather than an opportunity for further negotiations.

Mission

This term can be used to describe an embassy (headed by an ambassador) or a legation (headed by a minister). It is used as a general description of British representation in a particular country.

Note

In its most formal sense a communication from the head of mission to the government of the country in which it is situated. There are other types of note: 1) the collective note, which is addressed to a government by more than one representative on a matter of joint concern; and 2) the *note verbale*, which is more formal than a memorandum, but not as formal as a signed note.

Proces Verbal

The notes or minutes of a conference or congress. These may be signed by the participating representatives, in which case the conclusions are given added force. See *Acte Final*.

Protocol

A record of agreement, which has been increasingly used in the modern period as a basis for international decisions. Technically it does not have the same status as a treaty.

Treaty

Treaties can be bilateral (between two states), multilateral (between many) or of mutual guarantee.

20.4 Location of Documents Cited

The records described in this book can be consulted only at the following sites until the amalgamation of the records at Kew, expected in 1996/1997. Where a general group of records has been referred to in the text rather than a class (for example War Office or WO records), the list of locations provides a general reference to the lettercode. For information on the particular classes making up that group of records readers should consult Part 2 of the *Current Guide*.

CHANCERY LANE:

Chancery
C 47, C 54, C 61, C 66, C 70, C 71, C 76, C 181, C 187

Exchequer
E 30, E 36, E 39, E 101, E 351, E 403, E 404

Duchy of Lancaster
DL 34

Court of King's Bench
KB 33

Public Record Office classes (gifts and deposits):
PRO 30/5,PRO 30/15, PRO 30/24, PRO 30/25, PRO 30/26,
PRO 30/41, PRO 30/47, PRO 30/49, PRO 30/50, PRO 30/53;
(transcripts): PRO 31/1, PRO 31/2, PRO 31/3, PRO 31/4,
PRO 31/8, PRO 31/9, PRO 31/10, PRO 31/11, PRO 31/12,
PRO 31/13, PRO 31/14, PRO 31/18

Special Collections
SC 7

State Paper Office (state papers, foreign and domestic)
lettercode SP

Treasury Solicitor
TS 14, TS 26

KEW:

Admiralty
lettercode ADM

Agriculture, Fisheries and Food, Ministry of
lettercode MAF

Air Ministry
lettercode AIR

Audit Office
AO 1

Board of Trade
lettercode BT

British Council
lettercode BW

Cabinet
CAB 25, CAB 29, CAB 30, CAB 31, CAB 99, CAB 127,
CAB133, CAB 142

Colonial Office
lettercode CO

Defence, Ministry of
lettercode DEFE

Dominions Office and Commonwealth Relations Office
lettercode DO

Export Credits Guarantee Department
lettercode ECG

Foreign Office Records
lettercode FO
lettercode FCO (Foreign and Commonwealth Office)

Foreign Office intelligence records
HD 1, HD 2, HD 3, HD 4

German Foreign Ministry (captured documents)
lettercode GFM

Home Office
HO 37, HO 38, HO 168

Information, Ministry of
Lettercode INF

International organizations
lettercode DG

Overseas Development Administration/Ministry
lettercode OD

Paymaster General's Office
PMG 28

Prime Minister's Office
PREM 1, PREM 3, PREM 4, PREM 8, PREM 11

Public Record Office classes (gifts and deposits)
PRO 30/6, PRO 30/7, PRO 30/8, PRO 30/11, PRO 30/22,
PRO 30/29, PRO 30/30, PRO 30/33, PRO 30/36, PRO 30/
40, PRO 30/42, PRO 30/43, PRO 30/58, PRO 30/60, PRO
30/66, PRO 30/67, PRO 30/69.

Special Operations Executive
lettercode HS

Transport, Ministry of
MT 59

Treasury
T 1, T 48, T 75, T 78, T 144, T 194, T 225, T 232, T 234,
T235.

War Office
WO 309, WO 310, WO 311, WO 325, WO 331, WO 356,
WO 357

Index

The entries on this index refer to subjects, countries, people and other information which cannot readily be found from the contents listing. Headings or subjects marked in the contents pages have not generally been included. Information appearing in the appendixes has also been excluded.

C

D

L

M

N

82, 83, 85, 87, 97, 107, 110, 111, 165
  certified copies 20
  marriages 5, 20
  ratifications 5, 20, 44, 45, 82, 83
  warrants 83
  See also entry books
Treaty department 47, 62, 82, 83, 93, 95, 100, 113, 135
Treaty notes 18, 27
Treaty papers 18, 19, 46, 83, 135
Treaty rolls 5
Trevor, John 35
Turkey 50, 122; *see also* Ottoman Empire
Tuscany 18, 30
Tyrrell, Sir William 80

U

Ullswater, 1st viscount, *see* Lowther, J W
United Kingdom Commercial Corporation 103
United Kingdom Commissioner for Singapore and South East Asia 112
United Nations Organisation 56, 107-110
United Provinces 20, 27
Utrecht, treaty of 18

V

Vambery, Professor A 80
Venice 3, 4, 18, 30, 34, 38
Villiers, Sir Francis 80
Villiers, George, 4th earl of Clarendon 80

W

Wales
  marches 5
Walpole, Robert 35
Walsingham, Sir Francis 35

War Crimes trials 104, 105
War departments
  First World War 60, 101
  Second World War 101
War Office 90, 99
War Trade Department 100
War Trade Intelligence department 100, 101
Wardrobe 4, 6
Watson, Edward 80
Wellesley, Col. Frederick 81
Wellesley, Henry, 1st baron Cowley 81
Wellesley, Henry, 2nd baron Cowley 81
Western European Union 107, 109
White, Sir William 81
Whitworth, Charles, 1st baron 81
Wigram, Ralph 81
Williamson, Sir Joseph
  collection (SP 9) 11, 18, 27, 28, 35
Wilson, Sir Horace 81
Wilson, Thomas 11
Wiseman, Sir W 81
Wolsey, Cardinal 7, 32
Wood, Edward, 3rd viscount Halifax 81
Wotton, Sir Henry 36
Wriothesley, Sir Thomas 36
Wyndham, Charles, 2nd earl Egremont 36
Wyndham, W F 36
Wynn, Sir Henry 81